IDLENESS

IDLENESS

A PHILOSOPHICAL ESSAY

BRIAN O'CONNOR

PRINCETON UNIVERSITY PRESS

PRINCETON AND OXFORD

Copyright © 2018 by Princeton University Press

Published by Princeton University Press,
41 William Street, Princeton, New Jersey 08540

In the United Kingdom: Princeton University Press,
6 Oxford Street, Woodstock, Oxfordshire OX20 1TR

press.princeton.edu

Jacket image courtesy of Shutterstock

ISBN 978-0-691-16752-7

Library of Congress Control Number: 2018937064

British Library Cataloging-in-Publication Data is available

This book has been composed in Garamond Premier Pro
and Arial Rounded

Printed on acid-free paper. ∞

Printed in the United States of America

1 3 5 7 9 10 8 6 4 2

For Jane and Anna

CONTENTS

ACKNOWLEDGMENTS

It was a pleasure to work with Ben Tate of Princeton University Press, a source of good judgment ever since our very first discussions on the idea of a book about idleness. Fabian Freyenhagen, Owen Hulatt, Michael Rosen, †Liberato Santoro-Brienza, and Tom Stern were kind enough to offer a wide range of challenging criticisms as well as valuable suggestions for texts and passages I might consider. Many of the questions put to me by colleagues at various conferences and colloquia, my own university included, made their mark. Beth Gianfagna copyedited the manuscript with considerable diligence. As ever, though, my greatest debt is to Eileen Brennan for her endless insight and support.

IDLENESS

PHILOSOPHY AND IDLENESS

Questions about the nature of moral values predominate in philosophy's analysis of human action. There has been comparatively little concern with bringing to light assumptions about the kinds of people we are supposed to be in order to live as effective and happy actors within the highly integrated and productive societies of today. A moment's reflection makes it very clear that "fitting in" and "doing well" require us to be made—perhaps even, we might like to think, by our own free choices—into beings of a very specific and not obviously natural type. Among the key characteristics of this type is a reluctance to idle or a tendency to recognize some wrong in idleness even as we are tempted by it or succumb to it. Philosophers have weighed in with arguments designed to defend negative perceptions of idleness. Traditional moralistic rebukes of the idle are remodeled according to the latest notion of the greatness of humanity. Higher-level narratives about what we truly are or ought to be are offered in explanation of why idleness is not appropriate for beings like us. The aim of this study is to examine and ultimately to expose the presumptions and faults of those narratives.

I will eventually contend that idleness may, in certain respects, be considered closer to the ideals of freedom than the most prestigious conception of self-determination found in philosophy. This book, however, proceeds mainly by way of criticism and without advocacy for the idle life. This is not out of preference for either a superior stance of negativity or scholastic purism. Rather, positive recommendations risk underappreciating how deeply an ambivalence toward idleness is constitutive of much of what many of us take ourselves to be (a point that will be visited many times over the course of this study). That ambivalence will not be resolved by philosophical sketches of a life freed from the driving forces of industry.

Excluding a didactic and constructive approach does not, however, mean that the question of idleness exists here as a strictly theoretical problem.[1] The critical impetus is sustained by a sense of the harm our idleness-excluding-world does to human beings. That powerful anxiety, directly connected with the need to work for one's good standing, precariously serves our health and happiness. A social space within which a feeling of worth is gained by visible career and material success underwrites a peculiar vulnerability. Humiliation and trauma loom when the circumstances that enable realization of those goods are either only partially available to begin with or are suddenly taken from those who once enjoyed them. Suicide rates increase, families collapse, children struggle. A more stable and less ambitious socioeconomic system could possibly save us from some of the familiar perils of modern life. A bolder image of freedom is, though, offered by idleness. What that would look like in full is another kind of question. But one can conjecture that the genuinely idle would be spared the various forms of pain that are held in store even for those who try to make the most of the twinned institutions of work and social esteem. It is that very intuition that underpins the appeal of idleness even as it sits alongside the winning importance we ultimately attach to those institutions.

The notion of idle freedom—where work is no kind of virtue or path to worthiness—is meaningful and real enough to deserve protection. Here that protection will involve exposing the deficiencies of those many philosophical pronouncements in support of the official view of the world, the view that idleness is a bad, whereas busyness, self-making, usefulness, and productivity are supposedly the very core of what is right for beings like us. Exposing the assumptions and problems of the arguments against idleness might help to preserve the notion of freedom it embodies, even if it is mainly an oppositional freedom: liberation from those unsettling expectations that are all too difficult to resist. The main task of the book, then, will be, in a way, to prevent the philosophical case against idleness from having the last word. And we shall, in fact, see that philosophical accusations do not always lie so very far from more prosaic ones. The worries that, because of idleness, we are in danger of wasting our lives, of not doing justice to ourselves, or simply of not contributing are articulated in systematic and challenging forms in the texts to be considered. Some readers will not agree with my criticisms of those proposals that maintain that human beings are obliged to work toward something so much more impressive than idleness. Others may not believe they actually experience any desire for idleness—that, at least, is what I am sometimes told—and will therefore be unmoved by efforts in its behalf. This book does not hope to persuade them that they should think otherwise about whether they should develop that desire.

My critical approach could not be accurately described as balanced. I do not proceed with an open mind on whether or not idleness is a bad thing, and I am generally skeptical about any philosophical argument against it. Nevertheless, anti-idleness material is approached in the manner that seems to be expected by its authors. That is, I respond to the arguments found in those texts. I find almost none of them effective, for reasons that will become clear in the course of this book. Nor is my critical approach systematic. My various responses might conceivably amount to the basis of a different conception of work, happiness, or freedom. At this point a cohesive position is not, however, evident. Lastly, what is on offer here is not purely analytical in its dealings with its selected philosophers. Motivations as well as coherence will also be considered.

* * *

Idleness is a complex phenomenon whose meaning varies, sometimes quite radically, across contexts. The notion of idleness I want to explore encapsulates a form of experience that places us outside the norms or conventions of societies like ours. It is not only a state of not working, though that is a key marker. It involves a departure from a range of values that make us the kinds of people we are supposed to be in order to live well. The very idea of being a "self" of the appropriate kind is thereby placed in question. The features of the phenomenon of idleness—in the sense that is in focus here—can be roughly grouped. First, there are what we may label its *phenomenological features*, its distinctive feel. Idleness is experienced activity that operates according to no guiding purpose. That absence of purpose explains its restful and pleasurable qualities. Idleness is a feeling of noncompulsion and drift. We often become idle by slipping into it, either in the middle of tasks or for extended periods. The structure of our individual lives permits idleness in varying degrees, depending on the level of our commitments and the seriousness with which we take them. In principle, it is possible to imagine a life that is largely idle—that is, in which idleness is not a momentary release from work.

In this book, claims made against that possibility will be of special interest. Philosophers appear to express no worry about momentary or intermittent idleness, but a life of idleness is often seen by them as representative of humanity in a debased form.

A second dimension of idleness is its *effective* content. The activities that fill an idle period are not geared toward productivity. Should an interesting thought, of value to ongoing or future projects, arise during idleness, it is a serendipitous outcome. A further distinctive feature of idle behavior is its *structure*. It simply does not happen as a process involving disciplined self-monitoring. There is no sense of an inner power struggle in which something in us needs to be overcome or improved. Hence idleness, as we shall see, is perceived by its modern critics as an obstacle to some grand idea of self-realization. However, idleness is not mindless: no less than non-idle behavior, it contains conceptual components and judgments. As we idle we know what we are doing, even if we have no idea of an overall end or purpose in what we do. Idleness need not therefore be interpreted as essentially irrational. To construe it in that way is nothing more than to express the prejudice that rationality belongs to self-mastering, rule-guided actions only. Idleness, on the contrary, may offer a glimpse of an alternative way of living, one that looks wholly reasonable—makes sense—to those who experience it. It does, after all, seem to place us in a liberating possession of ourselves, free of

pressure, and evidently content. From these characteristics it is obvious that idleness stands in opposition to much of what is taken to be right and normal: it has nothing to do with performance, with
work, with social standing, with gaining in prestige.

Idleness can be found in other forms. Mannered
idleness—once theorized among a certain class as the
art of being idle—is quite different from the form described above. Mannered idleness is a way of life, carefully pursued and designed to create an impression of
effortless existence comfortably elevated above the
unintelligible toils of the masses. In its ostentation it
involves little or no weakening of a conventional social
sense. It wants to be seen and admired. That it is usually enabled by necessary social inequality—some will
work while others are seen to play—also separates it
from idleness in the sense that is implicitly dissatisfied
with the usual social arrangements.

It is important to distinguish the notion of idleness, as it will be studied here, from leisure. Idleness
obviously shares some of leisure's features. The
boundaries of leisure, though, are to be found in the
degree to which leisure can be incorporated within
the general model of the modern social actor. For
most who enjoy it, leisure is an instrument, allowing
us to cede temporarily from life-shaping demands.
Yet it is implicated in those demands. Leisure can
renew our capacity to perform. It allows us to recover
from labor or to think freely about our next task or
to augment ourselves by taking the trouble to gain

valuable new experiences (cultural tourism and the like). In today's world leisure may be considered a liberation of a sort, yet many labor regimes make leisure—paid vacation leave—obligatory. Leisure is good, apparently, not only for the worker but also for the employer. The general model of the effective social actor within a system of work is partly sustained in this way. Idleness, by contrast, threatens to undermine what that model requires, namely, disciplined, goal-oriented individuals. For that reason, idleness cannot be incorporated within the productivity model—unlike leisure—since it is a noninstrumental break from all that is required to make us useful. William Morris expressed a typical concern that leisure, which has become abundant in the modern world, should not be allowed to "degenerate into idleness and aimlessness."[2] Like numerous other social theorists, Morris speculated on the right balance between work and leisure. Too much leisure is idleness, a state of affairs in which no balance with work may be conceived, with imperiling consequences for the latter. In its indifference to productivity idleness clearly intersects with laziness. In some contexts—both critical and sympathetic ones—they are essentially synonyms. The family of Anna in Bertolt Brecht and Kurt Weill's *Seven Deadly Sins* cry out the traditional refrain that idleness is the beginning of all evil as they sing about the vice of laziness. Laziness is broadly perceived as a moral failing, as the state of a person who knows perfectly well what to do but who opts for rest anyway. In that specific sense, laziness can be separated from the implicitly critical or rebellious ways of idleness. In practice, though, no definitive demarcation between the two is to be found, and the notion of laziness will sometimes be in focus in the discussions of idleness that follow.

* * *

A history of idleness as a moral category would consider a range of similar-looking concepts that have emerged over its millennia-long history. Some discussion would need to be given, for instance, to sloth and *acedia*. This is not a work of genealogy, however. The focus of the analysis here is the distinctive way in which idleness comes into view in philosophy in what is broadly called the modern age. This is the age characterized by its interest in individual liberty, civic society, democracy, capitalism, and reason. Effective living within this world requires particular talents. We are expected to participate in its practices in various ways. We must develop skills that will prepare us for usefulness. Discipline is vital: we address our tasks with diligence and stand ready and willing for more. Disoccupation—idleness—is not an easy experience since our acquired discipline orients us towards yet more activity. Discipline here is not to be understood as task specific. That is, it does not refer to a situation in which one may take a highly structured approach to one's work or hobbies but be shapeless with regard to all else. Ideally our whole lives must take on a shape, a clear purpose, a "rational plan of life," as John Rawls calls it, which brings integrity to the totality of our actions. We are permitted to play, perhaps even to idle, but we will tend not to take up any of those options without considerable hesitation, since they run counter to the motivations that are normal for social agents like us. These moments of alternative living are not to be allowed to spoil the central project.

It should hardly be a surprise that the most significant *philosophical* considerations of idleness are found in our modern period. This is the era in which progress is directly connected with the efforts of human beings to bring reasoned order to the world. That order starts with the order we bring to ourselves. Idleness is obviously one kind of impediment to progress understood in that way. The contemporary age—modernity as some prefer to label it—is not, though, a monolith in which vital questions of what kinds of freedom, society, and humanity we want are settled or agreed. These notions are obviously subject to debate. Each theory of what we ought to be, nevertheless, understands itself as an advance on the world that has gone before. Rejections of archaic authority and hopes for a better type of humanity are shared. The specifics of each conception of freedom, society, and individuality demand, as we shall see, specific arguments against idleness.

* * *

A life marked by voluntary idleness could probably be described as hedonistic in the everyday sense of the word. With its indifference to planning, discipline, and usefulness, a life of that kind appears to be gratifying on its own terms, unmoved by those hard values that might be thought to give the modern world its peculiarly driving qualities. The perception of idleness within the technical sphere of *philosophical hedonism* is, however, a less straightforward matter. In principle, the academic form of hedonism should find no difficulty in acknowledging idleness as a perfectly satisfactory pleasure, and in that respect a preference that meets the warrant of morality (given the pleasure principle that serves as the normative source of philosophical hedonism). In fact, those acknowledgments are rare. One wholehearted example is to be found in David Hume's "The Epicurean." It is an effort to defend, what we might call, hedonic idleness and pleasure generally as the truest and most positive forms of human action. By looking at Hume's essay we can, at the outset of this study, address the question of whether the value of idleness is captured by philosophical hedonism and whether, therefore, the question of idleness can be left to a larger dispute about the moral status of pleasure.

Although "The Epicurean" lends support to hedonic idleness, it does not actually represent Hume's usual views of things. He generally has much to say against indolence. But a particular perspective is "personated"[3] in the essay in order to entertain the case for a life of pleasure within its defensible limits. Its sense of where those limits lie is of some interest. The essay takes as its enemy a philosophical claim that living according to certain "rules of reason" can generate a distinctive form of happiness, one that supposedly amounts to "a new pleasure." Hume voices the objection that the "original frame and structure" of human beings is not designed for such an unnatural variety of enjoyment. Rather, what pleases it is "ease, contentment, repose." This languid mode contrasts with the disagreeable regime of "watchfulness, care, and fatigue," which the proponents of a purely regulated life would inflict on us. The text speculates that "pride" motivates this effort to become self-sufficient, that is, independent of "the *outside*," but that independence is really nothing more than an exhibitionistic denial of pleasure. The "dictates of nature," it is confidently maintained, must win against the falseness of a life whose only basis is a "frivolous" philosophical theory.[4]

"The Epicurean" may seem to travel in the direction of everyday hedonism. A familiar constraining worry about hedonistic life, however, enters the discussion. Unfettered pleasure, we are told, exhausts itself. Now, in this context, the thesis has two main possible aspects. First, since pleasure is eventually expended, it cannot form the basis of any long-term way of life. It must therefore find its place among our other valuable activities. Or, second, pleasure is so great a good that it must guard against its overuse so that it can be enjoyed in the longer term. In fact, there are elements of both of these thoughts in Hume's essay. Pleasure should, it transpires, be controlled by "virtue," obscurely identified as its "sister." Pleasure checked by virtue will restore "to the rose its hue, and to the fruit its flavour." Through this partnership the "mind," as Hume carefully puts it, can keep "pace with the body." The wisdom we possess when in a state of virtuous pleasure can enable us both to repel "the barbarous dissonance of Bacchus" and to see through the absurdity of a life dedicated to the pursuit of glory at the expense of pleasure.[5]

In its efforts to give philosophical justification to pleasure and to bring it within the framework of morality, the stance of "The Epicurean" is perhaps less disruptive than it at first seems. In moderating pleasure with virtue, it implicitly rejects the idea that there is a good to be found in spontaneous indifference to what is expected of us. Rather, it recommends, among other things, an easeful life that can steer itself clear of scandal, that is, idleness in some way accommodated to virtue. Virtue excludes those options that entail an abandonment of all that is considered proper. Although its principles are not specified, it is clear enough that virtue has an authoritative normativity of its own. The recommendations of virtue are not subservient to the imperatives of pleasure. And virtue also contains a prudential function in ensuring that pleasure is not depleted. We get a sense from these various claims of where "The Epicurean" draws the limits to what human beings and their needs may be allowed to be. And among those needs, it appears, is moral justification. No form of pleasure deserves to be promoted if it transgresses the boundaries of what virtue can permit. "The Epicurean" gives rise to numerous questions about the coherence of at least this rather general variety of philosophical hedonism. The most obvious one is why pleasure is to be considered normatively significant given that pleasure must both be protected from itself and be subject to administrative overview by virtue. What is more relevant here, though, is whether the hedonic idleness that is valorized in "The Epicurean" really speaks to the sense of idleness we have so far considered. Hume's essay does not conceive of idleness in terms of freedom. It is considered, rather, as a pleasure in itself that may be morally licensed, not one that makes sense as a reaction to the world of busyness or the imperatives of self-making. In line with Hume's characteristic essentialism, it does not think that individuals are already constituted by those social conditions that make idleness both tempting yet almost impossible.[6] The idea of idleness as freedom, in comparison, is not the way of good sense. Certainly, that freedom is a pleasure, but it is one whose historical context gives it its content.

* * *

This contrast with philosophical hedonism may be even more sharply drawn by turning to one defense of idleness that amounts to an abandonment of the very idea of proper socialization and wise indulgence. This defense is significant in a further important way, since it is set against the demands of an incipient modern age. Friedrich Schlegel's Julius, in the philosophical novel *Lucinde* (1799), presents us with an "Idyll upon Idleness." He rejects the idea that idleness is *schole* ("leisure," pursued with virtue and for virtue). It should serve no end beyond itself. Idleness is rather, a "godlike art" of laziness and a "liberal carelessness and inactivity." Julius describes the general comportment of idleness as "passivity," in fact, as "pure vegetating [*reines Vegetieren*]," a descriptor Immanuel Kant will also use, as we shall later see. Schlegel contrasts the attitude of the idler with that of "self-conceit [*Eigendünkel*]," where the individual is caught up only in the imperatives of "industry and utility," which are darkly described as "the angels of death." Prometheus is identified as "the inventor of education and enlightenment" and also of the project, in effect, of a rational plan of life: "It's from him [Prometheus] that you inherited your inability to stay put and your need to be constantly striving. It's also for this reason that, when you have absolutely nothing else to do *you foolishly feel compelled to aspire to having a personality. . . .*" Julius, then, seems to be advancing the notion of idleness in a radical—socially critical—manner: (1) idleness defies industry, utility, and means and ends; (2) happiness is conceived as passivity rather than restless activity; and (3) idleness directs the individual away from what in more recent philosophy is called self-constitution (the task of making ourselves into integrated moral beings). Julius's critical insights against what he calls "Nordic barbarity" will have no little relevance in the theorization of idleness as a criticism of the modern social actor.[7]

Schlegel's language is striking and, in the use of the notion of "vegetating," perplexing. The metaphor could be unpacked in numerous ways. If it aims at describing our state of mind while idle, it is clearly excessive. Indeed, it does not match up with what we might imagine a "godlike art" to be. However, pitted against the notions of discipline and purpose, it has some purchase. It is keenly aware of its philosophical target: the ethics of Kant. And it differs from a more popular yet less radical appeal for idleness found in Jean-Jacques Rousseau's writings, which offer both influential ideas on social freedom (sometimes interpreted as the first articulations of the notion of autonomy) and deeply contrasting thoughts about a quasi-natural flight from purpose and opinion as freedom in some truer sense.

Rousseau's images of the freedom produced by uninhibited reverie lay claim to a form of idleness that is indifferent to opinion, albeit one that does not involve the abandonment of self-determination altogether. It is certainly not the kind of self-renunciation Schlegel entertains. Idleness of a particular type becomes possible, for Rousseau at least, when we can live in solitude in the countryside. In the *Confessions*, he declares: "The idleness [*l'oisiveté*] I love is not that of a do-nothing who stays there with his arms crossed in total inactivity and thinks no more than he acts. It is both that of a child who is ceaselessly in motion while doing nothing and, at the same time, that of a dotard who strays when his arms are at rest. I love to occupy myself by doing trifles, beginning a hundred things and finishing none of them . . . following only the caprice of the moment in everything."[8] Rousseau, as David James points out, develops a position in which freedom consists of "passively obeying a succession of impressions" rather than the familiar enterprise of concerted "self-direction."[9] Rousseau rather more famously finds freedom in the right kind of social organization, that is, in a community secured through the social contract, but here at least, the notion of freedom in the absence of others is explored. It is achieved by retreat from the critical and expectant gaze of society, away, indeed, from the city, "the abyss of the human species," as he puts it in *Emile*.[10]

Schegel, rather more audaciously, offers us not a rural adventure but a provocation that invites us to consider a kind of destruction of all the forces that draft out our lives for us. These forces may be experienced as standing in tension with a primitive desire to surrender to circumstances: "passivity"—a concept that is developed in the quite different space of Sigmund Freud's psychology. One way of understanding Freud's elusive notion of the death drive is as an analysis of the conditions in which the demands the ego places on the organism as a whole become unbearable. This motivates some attraction to a life without experience and, more specifically, one free from the pressure that reality brings with it. A tensionless state—which is death for the ego—can be gained by a dynamic release of the individual from the pressures of the ego: "The central and predominant intention of Thanatos, its aim and purpose, is precisely peace in one form or another, attained in some way or another."[11]

In "The Economic Problem of Masochism," Freud identifies three main drive principles—Nirvana, pleasure, and reality—allocating distinctive roles to each of them: "The Nirvana principle expresses the trend of the death instinct; the pleasure principle represents the demands of the libido; and the modification of the latter principle, the reality principle, represents the influence of the external world."[12] Pleasure and death each aim at a tensionless condition, whereas the reality principle forces the organism to forestall, painfully, that condition. The notion of a deathlike tensionlessness as some kind of reference point for idleness may seem far-fetched. And Freud's interest in this state is not to understand idleness but a specific pathological condition. The point will not be pushed hard in this book, notwithstanding Schlegel's intriguing language or Freud's fleeting insight. Nevertheless, it is clear that some of the most sophisticated criticisms of idleness find some use for analogies with unfamiliar and even non-human-like states of being when striking against human beings who have not learned—or who refuse—to make themselves useful or to keep themselves occupied. Some critics of idleness, in other words, mark out as failings some of the very things that proponents of idleness wish to emphasize as its advantages, namely, its destruction of what are considered the key markers of modern life. Included among those markers are activity, industry, planned self-realization, a firm sense of one's ego. The critics maintain that those in the supposedly awful condition of idleness lack the motivation to elevate themselves into a higher level of existence. That lack of motivation is, though, untroubled idleness: the human being who experiences no inner tension or self-alienation and, again, feels no urgency to have a "personality."

There is something disconcerting about the wholesale revisions in human reality that seem to come with a life of idleness. The much-valued ideal of "flourishing" might become an irrelevance, a thought that surely speaks against idleness. That ideal takes many forms. Martha Nussbaum, drawing lessons from the Athenians, has influentially explained it as a kind of harmony of virtue, excellence of character, and the freedom to participate in the politics of one's place.[13] The less classically minded will understand it as the exercise of freedom that sees individuals realize themselves in ways that personally enrich and please them. There is no agreement about the form flourishing ought to take. There is more likely to be convergence on when its possibility is precluded. Among the negative conditions standing in its way are political oppression, economic inequality, rigid class structures, limited access to education or food. If we think of flourishing as something that comes into view when negative conditions are in place, we might conclude that idleness need not be regarded as an impediment to it. Where idleness involves a way of living that has ceded from social pressures, thereby reducing the scope of the influence of socialization itself, it too may be understood as an expression of flourishing. Even, perhaps, the vegetating idler might be said to flourish insofar as that individual leads a life of a specific kind that is voluntary and that is fulfilled in its own terms. What would not count as flourishing would be the kinds of misery that accompany the effort to make something of ourselves in a world where success and triumphs of various kinds are accompanied by a worry about failure.

* * *

The texts examined in this book come mainly, though not exclusively, from the period of German idealism and its aftermath. But nothing here is examined for the sake of scholarship or historical commentary. A more important principle of selection is that the philosophers considered each articulate views of idleness that are now implicit, if not prevalent, in everyday discourse. They are undoubtedly more advanced and deeply grounded than common clichés about idleness and its dangers. But by looking closely at those views, we might hope to learn something about the kinds of justifications that are readily brandished whenever idleness becomes attractive.

The first chapter begins not with German philosophy or with philosophy at all but with a discussion of Robert Burton's analyses of idleness. We start there in order to establish what I take to be encompassed within premodern rejections of idleness. The model gleaned from Burton's work helps us to see what, in the sections that follow, is distinctive about Kant's later efforts to defend usefulness and rational self-determination. Kant's position may be cast in rather demanding theoretical terms but it aligns perfectly with a common view that a life worth living will be characterized by self-advancement and admirable industry. Kant, in fact, associates the attributes of usefulness and rational self-determination with "worthiness," a kind of inner quality that we have some obligation to realize. He maintains that the achievement of worthiness is not always pleasant or in line with our natural desire for idleness. It is nevertheless an ineluctable demand that is placed on us by virtue of the very beings we are.

G.W.F. Hegel, to whom I turn in the second chapter, takes a more integrationist view of human beings who have attained their worth. Nothing that we need to value is lost as human beings advance beyond the condition of savagery he finds among the peoples who still subsist in a state of idleness. He argues for the developmental advantages of those who can make themselves useful—even when there is no immediate use for them—and are able to contribute to the "system of needs" of all in a modern economy. As we shall see, a striking part of the story of this development is Hegel's identification of the formed or "educated" consciousness of a slave with the willingness to work usefully. Whereas Hegel's picture has something to do with what for him is the compelling dynamic of society, Karl Marx denounces idleness—a reluctance to work—on mainly moral grounds. It is a refusal to do what others need you to do, and it represents a retreat from the space of the "social" to selfishness. What is absent from Marx's account is a consideration of arrangements in which idleness—laziness, in his terms—is possible without some questionable reversion to isolated individuality.

The third chapter looks at the phenomenon of boredom as a consequence of idleness. In this perception of idleness we find no proposal for ennobling or positively liberating work. The philosopher who best represents this view is Arthur Schopenhauer. He argues that we are without the capacity for contented idleness. Our main task in life is to avoid idleness. We work, or throw ourselves into activities of virtually any kind, in order to escape the boredom that comes with idleness. This position represents a break from the idealizations of busyness found among Schopenhauer's illustrious predecessors. In a very important respect, however, it remains at a conventional level in that it does not consider whether our restlessness—our alleged incapacity for idleness—might be the product of social arrangements which form us in that way. Schopenhauer, rather, interprets human nature—though not always consistently—as fixed and ahistorical. The notion that boredom accompanies idleness is further illustrated in an examination of "the idle woman" offered by Simone de Beauvoir. Her position challengingly outlines the risk of boredom among individuals whose formation is not geared toward the realization of their actual needs.

Chapter 4 examines utopian efforts to reconcile the grim necessity of work with the distinctive freedom enjoyed in idleness. That reconciliation seems to promise to extricate human beings from Promethean burdens. It offers us the prospect that work might actually be a sphere of happiness rather than discipline and subordination to an alienating system. The models examined are those proposed by Friedrich Schiller and Herbert Marcuse, who both identify "play" as the space of this reconciliation. The obvious difficulties of giving coherent expression to what seems like a new harmony of extreme opposites will be examined. The book concludes, in chapter 5, with an assessment of the very idea of idleness as freedom. Idleness is contrasted with autonomy, a conception of freedom that continues to set the standards, among philosophers, of what freedom is supposed to be.

CHAPTER 1

OUR WORTHINESS FOR FREEDOM

Circumstances force most of us to take our lives seriously. We have to work hard in order to gain what we think we need and to protect the things that are important to us. In the context of pressing needs, idleness is a fantastic luxury. Our work, though, is not confined to basic security. General opinion about what counts as a proper life motivates, shapes, and justifies much of what we also do. The force of that opinion is difficult to resist. All sorts of labors are undertaken in the name of winning what only others can give us: standing, perhaps even prestige. Anyone who cannot acquire those "goods" is placed at a relative disadvantage to others. These kinds of life-consuming efforts have been neutrally framed as the attempt to acquire an "identity" through a "social role," that is, to become a person with a recognizable and socially effective character.

These days it is regarded as virtuous when we can be "pluralistic" about the different ways that people try to establish their identities as they pursue their preferred version of the good life. Each version has its own range of what is supposed to qualify as an impressive achievement. From outside their contexts, however, those very same achievements may appear trivial. Wealth, honors, cultivation, the right look might be everything to those who chase after them, whereas to others they are vainglorious or vacuous. Just occasionally we are jolted by the worry that those insults rightly apply to our very own personal passions. Humorous mockery of pretension and clumsy efforts at social elevation are found across Western literature. We laugh along, yet as one of its sharpest exponents discomfortingly observes, "Satire is a sort of glass, wherein beholders do generally discover everybody's face but their own" (Jonathan Swift, *Battle of the Books*). It is probably only those without a care for what they are who are safe from some satirical perspective. If there is absurdity in the human condition, it may not be down to some mismatch between our hopes and an indifferent universe. It is just as likely to be a matter of the comedy our lives provide for others.

One way or another, however, very few people are in any doubt about the challenges of managing the social pressures that hang over their lives. Even the occasional worry that there is nothing very valuable about our objectives does little to knock us off our stride. Yet in spite of all that, obvious though it is, there are philosophers who tell us that we do not take ourselves seriously enough. They blame all kinds of viciousness—

usually a cocktail of idleness and cowardice—for distracting us from the task of living in the right way. The right way involves some new and extreme manner of taking possession of ourselves. Philosophers with this message do not accept that we can either decently or intelligibly reject what they have to say to us.

Take the famous lecture that Jean-Paul Sartre gave in Paris on the theme of "existentialism as humanism" barely six months after the nightmarish war in Europe had concluded. He forcefully and repeatedly charged his audience, if not the world, with the offense of under-using and thereby misusing freedom. People were allowing others—political parties, religious institutions, social convention—to determine their values, choosing in that way to let others choose for them. They entered freely into these arrangements, but they were not acting freely enough. Human beings had to realize that what they choose, even when choosing indirectly, is always a matter for which they are answerable. And deciding one way or another could not, by its very nature, be easy. There are no codes or systems that exist independently of human action. Every choice creates an ethical principle. We must therefore approach each situation in anguish, unsure as to whether what we prefer to do is "the better," that is, what is best for humanity as a whole. Considerations of "the better" weigh heavily because each choice affects everyone else in bringing into existence a value that should, in principle, hold good for all: "In fashioning myself I fashion man."[1]

Was Sartre, as is commonly thought, attempting to reinvigorate European morality in the wake of its near extinction? Perhaps he himself saw it that way. But what is also interesting is that the core of his message had already been enunciated at least 150 years earlier, as we shall see in this chapter, under very different historical circumstances. It is essentially a thesis of the Enlightenment, and it continues to sustain the remarkable idea that we must build and perfect the self as an autonomous moral entity if we are to become properly human. In the current century, the same message has been adopted in a philosophical circle far from war and without a sense of the perilous state of Western values. Christine Korsgaard—whose views will be revisited in the concluding chapter of this book—believes that this work of making something of ourselves can be opposed only by some sort of pathology: "Timidity, idleness, and depression will exert their claims in turn" and prevent us from achieving what we supposedly know we must do.[2]

The line of thinking we find in Sartre and Korsgaard, among others, rests on a myth. Let us call it the worthiness myth. It is an uplifting story about how we human beings can overcome those human tendencies we take to be based in nature: the greater the effort, the more impressive and worthy the result. And it is this myth, perhaps more than any other assumed by philosophers, that has been used to deprive idleness of merit. How, those philosophers think, could we be so irresponsible as to turn away from the painful effort of elevating ourselves by preferring to idle? This question goes beyond condemnation of laziness or sloth. It rests on the relatively new idea of the obligation to become worthy of one's humanity through carefully chosen acts of self-realization.

The worthiness myth originates in this demanding form in Kant's efforts to articulate the hopes of the Enlightenment for his age. Nothing near to it is found among earlier theories of how we ought to live or, more significantly for this study, in accompanying accounts of the implications of refusing to do so. The novelty of this idea might be easier to appreciate if we take a contrasting look at Robert Burton's monumental *The Anatomy of Melancholy*, a work of the early seventeenth century. That book is unsparingly condemnatory of idleness, though not on the basis that it interferes with the pursuit of worthiness. Burton's worry relates to the consequences of idleness, and it is motivated by the view that human beings have a marked tendency to degenerate when idle. Once we have examined Burton we can, hopefully with sharper eyes, see what is distinctive about the Enlightenment criticism of idleness.

THE ANATOMY OF IDLENESS

Burton concludes his massive study with this advice for those who wish to avoid the torments of melancholy: "*Be not solitary, be not idle.*"[3] Early in the work, though, he is clear that, of the two states, there "is no greater cause of Melancholy then idlenesse."[4] At times idleness and solitariness are treated by him as part of a single phenomenon: they mutually imply one another. At other times they are independent causes of melancholy. A considerable amount of the book, in fact, teases out the exact nature of idleness's relation to melancholy. Burton's treatment of idleness can hardly be said to be either orderly or systematic, or directed even by a single line of thought, but it is certainly an effort to take a comprehensive view of the topic. From among his wide range of contentions, two enable us to gain a perspective on the historical shift in hostile views of idleness. The first—(1) below—lies in what Burton thinks of as the damaging consequences of idleness. The second—(2) below—focuses on the kind of idleness that he believes to be peculiar to the aristocratic classes. The first of these contentions will provide us with a vantage point from which to consider contrastively Enlightenment claims about the inherently unworthy character of idleness. And Burton's criticisms of aristocratic idleness show us that there are accounts of what it means to be vigorously active, yet viciously idle. The vice does not amount to a lack of productivity, but to the lack of a directed effort. Burton, in fact, has a great deal to say in support of productivity, but he does not think of its absence as equivalent to idleness.

(1) Burton divides his analysis between physical and mental forms of idleness. Although physical idle-

ness, he holds, tends to cause unenviable digestive disorders, its effects are not limited to the body. It is, he writes, "the nurse of naughtinesse, stepmother of discipline, the chiefe author of all mischiefe, one of the seaven deadly sinnes, & a sole cause of this and many other maladies, the Divels cushion."[5] Burton is following conventional moral teaching when thinking of idleness as a space within which wickedness can take hold. Even the very difficult notion that idleness actually *causes* mischief is a commonplace among those contemporaries and predecessors of Burton whose moral beliefs were marked by the Christian tradition.[6] That thought rests on the view that human beings are prone to degeneracy. Little effort is required to lapse into that vicious state. Idleness clearly offers no resistance to that propensity.

Burton, though, has a more ambitious theory to add to the received wisdom. Namely, that idleness produces damaging mental disturbances. The idle mind, he writes,

> macerates and vexeth it selfe with cares, griefes, false-feares, discontents, and suspicions, it tortures and preyes upon his owne bowels, and is never at rest. This much I dare boldly say; he or shee that is idle, be they of what condition they will, never so rich, so well allied, fortunate, happy, let them have all things in abundance, all felicity that heart can wish and desire: all contentment, so long as he or she, or they are idle, they shall never be pleased, never well in body and

minde, but weary still, sickly still, vexed still, loathing still, weeping, sighing, grieving, suspecting, offended with the world, with every object, wishing themselves gone or dead, or else carried away with some foolish phantasie or other.[7]

The mind, it seems, has a way of attacking the happiness of those with the tendency to ruminate and who are also without distraction from troubling, and eventually, self-perpetuating negativity. This latent capacity for self-destruction from within also allows us to understand how solitariness, as Burton and others have thought, could contribute to melancholy. Isolated from others, a person is more inclined to become absorbed in lonely and troubling thoughts. It is notable, though, as we shall see through Kant, that Enlightenment philosophy has the quite different worry that idleness is a far too enjoyable way of living, and it threatens not so much our organic existence or happiness but our higher selves.

(2) A recurrent theme in Burton's account of idleness is that it is a distinctive luxury for those included among the nobility. Indeed he sees physical idleness as "the badge of gentry."[8] He does not at the same time think of the aristocratic class as slothful, that is, physically inactive. Their idleness appears to consist in their liberty to avoid real work. And they use their time, instead, with a concerted commitment to play. Their dedication to "sports, recreations, and pastimes," physically demanding though they might well

be, can be counted as idleness. What separates these exertions from the more acceptable ones is that they are not stimulated by a "vocation." Because it is without vocation, play is somehow pointless and, on that basis, idle. This distinction is hardly watertight when applied to the two spheres. Burton tries to help us by stipulating that activity of a vocational kind involves taking "paines" in pursuit of some meaningful ends.[9] But this does not really separate it from the riotous though skilled pleasures of "hawking, hunting, &c. & such like disports and recreations." Burton is left simply with an asserted and conventional exclusion of those pleasures from the category of "honest labour."[10]

More significant, though, is that what counts as honest labor, in fact, is not equivalent to productivity. Among Burton's recommendations "to expell Idlenesse and Melancholy" is intensive study. Clearly, this reflects the preference of a bookish man like Burton. He cites, with agreement, a well-known line from Seneca's eighty-second epistle: "*To be at leasure without bookes is another hell, and to be buried alive.*"[11] He does not seem to follow the view Seneca puts forward in *De otio* that studious contemplation, and a leisurely withdrawal from civic life, can lead to an enhancement of the republic. In that essay, Seneca posits the idea of a republic that is not reducible to the existing arrangements of the state. He is speaking about the kinds of ideal political actor that we may sometimes be able to become only when we have the freedom to spend our time in philosophical reflection. We can be theorists when we no longer have to compromise our principles to meet the needs of everyday politics. Seneca writes that this "greater commonwealth [*res publica*] we are able to serve even in leisure [*in otio*] . . . so that we may enquire what virtue is. . . ." For that reason he rejects the charge that he is recommending contemplation for its own sake: "[W]hen virtue is banished to leisure without action it is an imperfect and spiritless good, that never brings what it has learned into the open."[12] Withdrawing from the demands of everyday life and turning toward leisurely contemplation turns out to be of eventual benefit to the political actor. Seneca's clarification that contemplation is "spiritless" if it does not inform the way we live makes a claim that might have been of service to Burton. It could have provided him with a decisive way of distinguishing between intensive study and intensive leisure. The "vocation" of the former in Seneca's text is its contribution to a better state. Instead, Burton leaves his own preference for studiousness without a secure principle with which to distinguish it from concerted leisure.

Burton's recommendation, in contrast with Seneca's, appears mainly to be that we use study to occupy the mind and keep it disciplined by undertaking difficult tasks. Those tasks, it seems, may indeed bring us closer to the divine, but their main objective is to preserve us from melancholy. Burton warns us that "overmuch study" can also be destructive. Taken to excess, study becomes a form of solitariness that, again, induces melancholy. Women, Burton thinks, must protect themselves from melancholy by different means: they should undertake "insteed of laborious studies . . . curious Needle-workes, Cut-workes, spinning, bone-lace, and many pretty devises of their owne making, to adorne their houses, Cushions, Carpets, Chaires, Stooles . . . confections, conserves, distillations, &c. which they shew to strangers. . . ." A final point to draw from Burton's conception of the non-idle occupations is that neither study nor the decorative arts are productive in the economic sense. What is produced through them is confined either to the scholar's mind or to the home: the community at large does not stand to gain, at least in Burton's account. What is valuable in these activities is primarily that they demand dedication, give those who undertake them an inner repose, distracting them from self-destructive thoughts. Idleness induced melancholy and mischief are kept at bay. Burton, though, takes that last idea to an extreme. At one point—and not obviously ironically—he effectively suggests that it may be beneficial for idlers to have tasks imposed upon them. He offers the case of the Israelites who, apparently, were so little burdened by the Egyptians that they could idly contemplate rebellion. By heaping more work upon his slaves the Pharaoh, Burton says, cured them of their idleness and extinguished the mental space within which discontent could foment a demand for liberation.[13]

From Burton's view of idleness we can abstract the implicit but philosophically archaic conception of the human being that supports it. Our human existence seems to be shaped both by the force of an original tendency to destroy ourselves and our best efforts to fight against that tendency. In this context, the idler is effectively allowing that latent destructiveness to take hold. This process is conceived to accord with the doctrine of original sin: "that generall corruption of mankinde," Burton calls it.[14] Idleness means succumbing to sin. This, in fact, echoes a point earlier asserted by Calvin. He thinks of the virtuous life as one of strict discipline, and the absence of discipline as the descent into moral decay. He writes: "It just happens to it as with refractory horses, which, if kept idle for a few days at hack and manger, become ungovernable, and no longer recognize the rider, whose command before they implicitly obeyed."[15] For Burton, the successful fight against idleness also means the pursuit of virtue. Virtue, in this context, will not be the positive realization of our higher essence, some project through which we establish our worthiness. It is, less heroically, the development of a character capable of resisting sin. This involves commitment to tasks that meet the criteria of being a "vocation." It does not rest on a very cheerful view of humanity. That should not surprise us, given its view of original sin, in which human beings exist between irredeemable corruption and the gruelling fight against corruption. A more optimistic view of what human beings might make of themselves, as we shall see, transformed some of the elements implicit in accounts, like Burton's, of the evils of idleness.

KANTIAN WORTHINESS

Kant does not offer a general account of idleness, but where it does appear in his writings he is usually attempting to make an important and positive point about what human beings ought to try to be. Although he emphasizes the exertions required to bring about a higher state of positive human virtue—not merely avoidance of vice—he is sharply at odds with an equally influential view that work itself is the source of virtue. Among some of Kant's contemporaries—writers of the Scottish Enlightenment—there was the view that *homo sapiens* is also, essentially, *homo laborans*.[16] As such, work is not just a practical necessity, an unwelcome but unavoidable means of survival; it is the proper realization of an inner essence of human beings. Adam Ferguson, for example, argued that a preference for idleness seemed valid only if the work available was not attractive enough. The wrong kind of work would always be experienced as limiting. Commonly, that negative experience has been falsely taken to be an essential feature of work: "The person who is thus confined, without being occupied, mistakes his aversion to confinement for an aversion to business; and his longing for a change of occupation

he mistakes for a dislike to exertion."[17] The right kind
of work, by contrast, should be more truly desirable
than idleness because it, above any other activity,
could fulfill the worker. Kant also believes that labor
is a good thing, though not because he is generally interested in the economic conception of human beings.
Officially, he is not. The thought that shapes his view
of idleness, rather, is that it is an unworthy way of life
for beings like us. What makes us worthy involves
both self-development and our development of the
social world. These tasks require a certain kind of effort. That effort may not always please us, but no rational grounds could give us reason to avoid it. A life
of ease is possible only when we choose to take no active part in influencing the world around us. In that
unfortunate case, though, we leave the world as we
find it, as overprotected children do. Our rational nature means that we ought not to retreat from the challenge of self-realization, of taking full possession of
ourselves as rational moral beings (not, therefore,
purely as economic beings).

What Kant proposes is a self-consciously historical
claim. It is, he knows, appropriate to the age in which
he is living, not an abstract thesis about human beings
at all times and in every circumstance. The prospect of
Enlightenment had come into view, allowing human
beings, finally—as the progressive interpretation
would see it—to realize themselves individually as autonomous beings and, collectively, as a rational community. Idleness, in this light, is a denial of Enlighten-

ment. It amounts to a refusal to meet the challenge of taking responsibility for oneself and the institutions of the state. This resistance would have to be named and discredited if progress is to be maintained. That mission threads itself through three works, which Kant produced within a few years of each other, on the prospect of an enlightened world: "An Answer to the Question: What Is Enlightenment?" (1784), "Idea for a Universal History with a Cosmopolitan Purpose" (1784), and *Groundwork of the Metaphysics of Morals* (1785).

Idleness versus Maturity

Kant opens the essay on enlightenment with the provocation that the hallmark of enlightenment is the courage to think for oneself. That thinking for oneself has, at that point in history, become a general possibility for all human beings means, at last, that the species stands at the threshold of maturity. Kant notes that we do not quite live "in an *enlightened* age . . . but we do live in an age of *enlightenment*." There are still many who have yet to demonstrate a willingness to develop their capacity for independent-mindedness. Individuals with that capacity will act only in accordance with principles that they can recognize as rational law. A rational law is never based on sentiment, taste, personal interest, or external authority. Dogmas and traditional rules can have no power over beings who have learned how to govern themselves through reason. That does not necessarily mean, though, that some of the content of tradition and custom might not be salvageable by means of the right kind of analysis. Standing in the way of an "enlightened age," however, are the idle and the weak. Kant writes: "Laziness and cowardice are the reasons why such a large proportion of men, even when nature has long emancipated them from alien guidance, nevertheless gladly remain immature for life." Human beings need to be freed from the infantilizing lessons and warnings of failure that they hear from the ruling voices. As things stand, only exceptional individuals have gained the power of genuine self-determination. Once alerted to the modern truths of human potential, everyone, though, has a duty to contribute to the intellectual liberation of humanity, that is, to ensure that the historical project of enlightenment is maintained for others: "A man may for his own person, and even then only for a limited period, postpone enlightening himself in matters he ought to know about. But to renounce such enlightenment completely, whether for his own person or even more so for later generations, means violating and trampling underfoot the sacred rights of mankind."[18]

The notion of a historical project, arduously pursued, is framed in a broader way in Kant's essay on "Universal History." There Kant investigates the possibility that the apparently individually motivated and self-serving actions of separate human beings might, ultimately, conform to some sort of plan for humanity of which individuals are themselves unaware. The case is made through a number of theses, the first and second of which together hold that rationality is a special capacity of human beings, a capacity that can be fully realized through the species as a whole, not by any single individual. The short duration of human life explains why the full realization of human rationality by individuals is precluded. (Kant is therefore not saying that reason is an intersubjective achievement; that is, one which rests on processes of communal mutuality and reciprocity. It seems, rather, that reason grows, and that growth is passed along the generations.) The prospect for the species of establishing a fully completed rationality is thought of by Kant as an objective way of justifying the continuing endeavor and progress of human rationality. He makes a remarkable connection between that endeavor and the everyday reality of rationality. His claim is that we would not be right to see ourselves as rational beings if rationality was not capable of eventual perfect realization. And in this case "all practical principles would have to be abandoned, and nature, whose wisdom we must take as axiomatic in judging all other situations, would incur the suspicion of indulging in childish play in the case of man alone."[19] This is an unbearable thought, and on that basis, it appears, it is taken to be false. It is implicit, then, that progress toward completed rationality is part of the function of individual acts of rationality.

The gradual realization of reason by the species sees us slowly supersede our original "basic animal equipment" as we develop talents and skills through our own freedom.[20] It follows, Kant believes, that we human beings are ultimately dissatisfied with any arrangement for which we are not responsible. Paradisal comforts are not for us, no matter how much they may appeal to our imaginations. It does not lie in our fundamental nature that we can enjoy this life without having made it a life that can be enjoyed. The emphasis here, in fact, is on the making rather than on the enjoying. Idle rest has no importance alongside that objective. Furthermore, our efforts to establish a world in which pleasure finally triumphs is a delusion: what we more deeply enjoy is trying to make that world. Kant writes: "Yet nature does not seem to have been concerned with seeing that man should live agreeably, but with seeing that he should work his way onwards to make himself by his own conduct worthy of life and well-being."[21] Unworthiness, it would seem to follow, is a preference for actions that are free of any implicit consideration of how one should "work" oneself "onwards."

Kant sees the human being as a contradictory creature, as a kind who prefers easy comfort but who is at the same time also driven by a rational nature to "abandon idleness [*Lässigkeit*] and inactive self-sufficiency and plunge instead into labour and hardships, so that he may by his own adroitness find means of liberating himself from them in turn."[22] We saw

Kant's worry that nature would be "indulging in childish play" were our rational deeds not ultimately a contribution to the development of rationality in the species. But the view he expresses here would surely make the urge for rational action into another kind of tormentor: we would continually abandon idleness in order to give ourselves burdens that we sought to overcome. It is, however, precisely this torment that accompanies the worthiness myth: the importance of the endeavor to make ourselves independent of natural or settled circumstances, regardless of the attractions of idleness and other pleasures.[23]

The emergence of society as a whole is also connected with the achievement of individual worthiness. Ordered community appears to be produced as a response to the experience of opposition among human beings. In the face of antagonism, the individual had better, simply to survive, "overcome his tendency to laziness."[24] However, something more than an uneasy peace is established through that effort. In finding solutions to our unsocial sociability, "the social worth of man" is gained. That worth is fundamentally incompatible with idle pleasure. Nothing can be achieved in idleness, and foolish ideas about a properly human life that does not develop through competition is dismissed as naive. Once again, then, at a crucial point Kant ties his hopes for human progress to a denigration of blissful inactivity: "Without these asocial qualities (far from admirable in themselves) which cause the resistance inevitably encountered by

each individual as he furthers his self-seeking preten-
sions, man would live an Arcadian, pastoral existence
of perfect concord, self-sufficiency and mutual love.
But all human talents would remain hidden for ever in
a dormant state, and men, as good-natured as the
sheep they tended, would scarcely render their existence more valuable than that of their animals. The
end for which they were created, their rational nature,
would be an unfilled void."[25]

The idler, in this world, drops to the level of a passive beast. Active human beings, by contrast, negotiate
the antagonistic tendencies of both themselves and
others. And while pursuing the immediate task of re-
solving antagonism, they actually bring humanity ever
closer to reason. Selfishness is never overcome, but it
is accommodated as the stimulant for the realization
of rationality. This competitive environment, with
human beings inclined nevertheless to live cheek by
jowl, gives every motivation for a disciplined and determinate progress. That is the supposed advantage of
civilization. Without the motivation of competition,
we are likely to be ill-formed: "In the same way, trees
in a forest, by seeking to deprive each other of air and
sunlight, compel each other to find these by upward
growth, so that they grow beautiful and straight—
whereas those which put out branches at will, in freedom and in isolation from others, grow stunted, bent
and twisted."[26] In the case of human beings an isolat-
ing freedom might be either a matter of circumstances
or of preference. As a preference, though, it is a viola-

tion of our obligations, as creatures capable of rationality, to the development of a fully rational species. This thing of beauty is born of strife. What is difficult to see in this, though, is how the same basic tendency to strife can become the engine of worthiness unless social progress effects a permanent change in the human character. That change would see human beings lose their competitive striving. But Kant does not appear to think this. Instead we are left with more or less organized societies driven by the same aggressive energies. In this context, rationality means taking possession of ourselves, developing principles that move us beyond the realm of nature. This series of claims provides Kant with a set of background concepts with which to dismiss idleness as a legitimate preference.

The Unworthy Idler

In the *Groundwork of the Metaphysics of Morals*, Kant sets out to demonstrate why the "universal imperative of duty" is compelling for human beings considered as rational beings. This imperative holds: "act as if your maxim were to become by your will a universal law of nature."[27] What this means, in effect, is that we should select only those rules of action that could have validity for everyone. The more we universalize the actor—that is, focus on common characteristics alone—the less we can prefer our individual perspectives. People differ in their sentimental attachments and emotional

responses. "Feeling," therefore, cannot be the basis of
a moral law, since the content of any feeling is a matter
of individual reaction. It is, though, in the nature of a
law that it appeals impartially to each person as a
moral agent, rather than as a specific person with situated
interests. In Kant's view, it is the rational side of
our humanity that is our common core.

Kant explores the case of an idler who shows no
inclination to cultivate a talent that would "make him
a human being useful for all sorts of purposes."[28] For
reasons that Kant does not explain, this man is now
willing to gauge whether his idleness might be consistent
with the universal imperative of duty, an imperative
that up to this point has had no evident appeal for
him. This would seem like too much effort for someone
who had already lived well and in his own way.
Kant brings two assumptions to this fictional scenario.
First, he imagines that his idler is amenable to the
kinds of reasons for action Kant favors: the universalizable
principles that an autonomous being can construct
and defend. But it is more likely that the idler is
motivated primarily by what gives him individual satisfaction
in any given situation. The demand of autonomy,
that we are willing to defend our actions with
reasons, is attractive when that demand is placed on
individuals who have authority over us. But why
would or should individuals with harmless ideas of
how they will live be obliged to reason with anyone?
The second assumption is that the idler finds something
interesting in the question of what kind of per-

son he would make of himself. The business of worthiness begins to enter the picture. Kant believes that, ultimately, the idler could not defend his drifting existence. As a rational being he would appreciate that his self-neglect was unsustainable. We have already seen, in the "Universal History" essay, what that unsustainability consists in: our rational human nature drives us to invent challenges for ourselves, and the successful negotiation of those challenges produces a worthy person, if not a community.

In the *Critique of Practical Reason*, Kant tries to explain how we are motivated to achieve worthiness in spite of the ways it opposes our tendencies to idleness and pleasure generally. He argues that reason rather than desire provides us with the very possibility of the kind of freedom that counts. In answer to the question of how such a dismal course could ever recommend itself to idle creatures—whose freedom is not a matter of self-discipline under principles that are valid for all—Kant also claims that we are in some sense compensated for the unpleasantness that goes with acting under laws that control our desires by a cognitive gain in our appreciation of ourselves. He sets out that idea as follows: "As *submission* to a law, that is, as a command (indicating constraint for the sensuously affected subject), it therefore contains in it no pleasure but instead, so far, displeasure in the action. On the other hand, however, since this constraint is exercised only by the lawgiving of his own reason, it also contains something elevating." This emotionless sense of elevation may attend doing "what one does not altogether like to do."[29] This reluctance, Kant seems to concede, is a necessary feature of the exercise of that freedom which grants us a sense of "greater inner worth."[30]

Kant willingly accepts that it is possible to imagine a world in which most people would lead idle lives. This is indeed evident, according to Kant, in exotic places: "(as with the South Sea Islanders) the human being should let his talents rust and be concerned with devoting his life merely to idleness [*Müßiggang*], amusement, procreation—in a word to enjoyment."[31] The South Sea Islanders, perhaps among others, are somehow not subject to that driving process of nature that, we have seen Kant claim, does not allow "man" to "live agreeably." Indeed, we also saw that Kant regards it as a travesty when human potential is neglected in favor of Arcadian idleness. Rather, "we" are made in such a way that our only true satisfaction is gained from advancing our circumstances through effort. The idleness of alien cultures can give us no insight into how we might live: their arrangements, apparently, are without relevance for us. We are beings who are more profoundly amenable to the claims that reason places on the decisions we make about our lives. A rational being, Kant believes, would never will that idleness become a "universal law." Of course, a rational being could consider that possibility. But that person would ultimately see that idleness could not be a law for all rational beings, since such a way of life is a matter of personal disposition, a preference of a particular type of person. The evidence from the blissful lives of the South Sea Islanders would carry no weight in favor of such a law. Kant also maintains that a rational being, which he seems to conceive as a philosophically capable person, would not wish to see idleness as a rule "be put in us as such by means of natural instinct."[32] In that state of affairs rational beings would no longer pursue any means of becoming worthy of their humanity: they would effectively cease to be rational beings as such. Kant believes that each person has a variety of talents that can be adapted to make the most of the surrounding world. These talents "serve him and are given to him for all sorts of possible purposes."[33] To wish that human beings become idlers by nature is to entertain the circumstances in which those talents would have little prospect of development.

Although Kant's line against the idler appears to fit neatly with his notion of human progress through restless endeavor, a second and slightly different consideration is implicit in the argument of the *Groundwork*. The claim of "Universal History," as we saw, is that new talents emerge as human beings respond to an inner need to gratify themselves both by making the world around them and by negotiating their way through mutual antagonism. The *Groundwork*, however, casts the idler in a different context. The idler has the potential to contribute to the world in which he finds himself: he is, after all, "a human being useful for all sorts of purposes." If the idler is to be persuaded that he should change his way of life, though, he will need to understand what it is to be useful. Would he be compelled by the argument that human progress requires his services? That can hardly be Kant's point. Instead, the lever must be that the idler is convinced that he can have that special feeling of worthiness if he makes himself useful within the society around him. What is to count as useful is not always, if ever, within the power of any one individual. We become useful in accordance with the needs of whatever community we happen to be in. This gives rise, though, to the question of whether Kant has decided to elevate the practices of conventional society to the status of what is rational, since making oneself useful is taken by him as a sign of the exercise of rationality. If that is the case, then one of the motivations behind the criticism of idleness is laid bare. The idler is in opposition to, what some have called, the "second nature" of social practices. He is unmoved by the conventional measure of what will make him a better type of person. Kant makes a remarkable connection between that measure and rationality.

One way or the other, the idler is certainly unworthy of himself. He disavows his useful capacities, though not those that give him pleasure, and this is an irrational defiance of what he ought to be. Kant never suggests that the idler is a danger to himself. He does not offer us a portrait of mental, moral, or physical degeneracy resulting from idleness. His emphasis on the inherent irrationality of idleness sets him far apart from the idea exemplified in Burton that idleness is to be avoided because of its consequences. Kant momentarily beguiles us with the vision of the contented South Sea Islanders. But he tears us away from those Islanders by reminding us of our obligations to ourselves. Whether we are moved by that reminder depends on how deeply we have come to accept the idea of making ourselves worthy. It is that idea alone which serves as Kant's bulwark against idleness. This idea is by no means an eccentricity of Kant's peculiar worldview. It is a profound theoretical justification of an idea that has now become commonplace: that a life worth living is one marked by effort and achievement. Kant would like to think that "worthiness"—the idea that holds so many of his claims together—is not a transient value. The pursuit of worthiness, we have seen him argue, is inscribed in us by nature. What overshadows this claim, however, is Kant's association of worthiness with usefulness, once we think of usefulness as a property whose practical intelligibility depends on contingent historical needs.

I have argued that the imperative that we make ourselves worthy of our true selves attempts directly to denigrate idleness as a way of living. And I have claimed that this imperative is a myth. Its mythic character becomes evident in the tensions between the ways in which the material is determined and the ways in which it is defended. The notion that the pursuit of worthiness grounds a range of human endeavors is the central element of Kant's theory of self-making. However, his analyses never manage to settle the account in favor of that belief. The belief, though, is not surrendered or modified. We have seen that Kant is committed to the idea that human beings will only realize their full potential through effort. Furthermore, striving toward that realization is preferable to human beings, understood as rational beings, to the easy pleasures of the idler. But in each of the arguments Kant provides for this idea, rationality proves to be elusive. Kant frequently admits that human beings find little to complain about in the idle life. It is only when the notion of the rational being is dangled in front of them that they become unsettled. But what is gained through that interference? Furthermore, why is that interference even required if it is in the nature of human beings to eschew the comforts of a settled and unchallenging existence? Another worry is that reason looks more like expedience or pragmatism when its full realization is found in the resolution of social antagonism. The societies we create to satisfy our twin urges for sociability and competitiveness stand as solutions to the problem of violence. In several instances we have seen Kant connect rationality—the determined self-realization of one's talents—with the needs of historical circumstances. The result is the reduction of our efforts to the needs of an environment that precedes us. None of these ideas and arguments demonstrate that human beings prefer to transcend themselves in order to become worthy of their higher

humanity. Most troubling of all, that notion of worthiness gives legitimacy to the idea that striving and
becoming useful are superior to mere idleness. It is an
insistent stipulation through which experience is reor-
ganized into a notional hierarchy.

Bildung

Kant's thinking on the positive relationship between
freedom and usefulness might be thought to compli-
cate his fundamental moral precept that we should be
treated as ends and never as means. To gear our lives
toward usefulness places us at the mercy of ends that
are determined by others. There is, nevertheless, a
quite significant idea at stake in what Kant, among a
number of other Enlightenment thinkers, is trying to
do: his effort is to narrow, if not nullify, the gap between individual freedom and the ordinary require-
ments of everyday life. The ideal of a reconciliation of
freedom with social existence would later be pursued
on quite different grounds in the post-Kantian social
theories of Hegel and Marx.

Among Kant's contemporaries there were some
who did not, however, believe that this particular reconciliation was of any value. Indeed, from one perspective it represented a tawdry compromise in which
the boundless possibilities of individual self-
development were ultimately impaired by the anony-
mously declared needs of the world. The name of this

process of self-development is *Bildung*. The word *Bildung* has a long and enduring history within German thought, indicating in its main usages education as ordinarily understood or, more broadly, formation through cultural experience. A more rarefied sense—the one of interest here—gained currency at around the very time Kant was making claims for usefulness as a kind of rational freedom. This very specific sense of *Bildung* emerged from an earlier religious idea that Christians should endeavor to make—to form, *bilden*—themselves in the image of Christ. It follows from being a Christian that one could find no better way of life than that lived by Christ himself. The *imitatio Christi* imperative does not rest on the idea that Christ exemplifies certain moral or spiritual goods. That idea, after all, is not beholden to the full authority of revelation. Rather, according to one line of Christian thought, each human being as a "copy [*Abbild*]" of an "original [*Urbild*]" ideal should strive to become like that ideal.[34] This notion implicitly requires that individuals elevate themselves above the coarse purposes of society.

One consequence of extracting this ideal of perfectibility from its original religious end is to deprive it of a specific model to emulate. The criterion of perfection becomes less clear, since once secularized it cannot be represented in a divine being. Correlatively, imitation of a non-divine being would be mere copying. Perhaps we should not then be surprised at a vagueness that surrounds the ends toward which *Bil-*

dung directs us. When the philosophers and other writers of Kant's time embraced the notion of *Bildung* as self-development, they proposed, as Humboldt put it in a work of 1792, that "originality" could be gained through a combination of "individual vigour" and "manifold diversity."[35] The product of this enterprise would be unique. Originality could not be modeled in advance, nor could individuals be instructed by others in how they might find their own particular form of living. Little extended or overlapping articulation of what *Bildung* could concretely add up to can be found among the writers with whom this notion is generally associated.[36] One feature, though, is certainly common to the most demanding notion of individual *Bildung*. In it there is an absolute opposition between the good of maximal self-realization and the need to be useful, or "external ends."[37] Usefulness means nothing more than a brutal sacrifice of individuality, regardless of any other advantages it may promote.[38] This precious view of the self also sees threats in the idea of universal moral laws, since they necessarily obligate individuals to realize themselves within a common and predictable space. *Bildung* in its purest form may then lead individuals toward inwardness, since it involves, as Thomas Mann observed, "consideration for the careful tending, the shaping, deepening and perfecting of one's own personality."[39] This self-fashioning might be a purely individualistically conceived, realized, and maintained unification of mind, body, and emotion.[40] It could also be described as the harmonious expansion of the personality achieved through constant effort.[41] This extraordinary responsibility to oneself requires the most demanding self-involvement.

Even among those writers who took a less aggrandizing view of *Bildung* it is evident that idleness cannot prevail as a permanent mode of experience. In *Wilhelm Meister*, the eponymous hero and his traveling companions find themselves enchanted at one point by "the delicious economy of a band of gipsies . . . entitled to enjoy in blissful idleness [*in seligem Müßiggange*] all the adventurous charms of nature." This comfort could not, however, last: "activity awoke among the younger part of them."[42] The episode that leaves Wilhelm physically injured begins with the theatrical and purposeless combat of the players, but immediately gives way to the intrusive violence of the real world. After recovery, Wilhelm does not try to return to the lost ways of idleness. Rather, he "proposed no more to lead an aimless routine of existence: the steps of his career were henceforth to be calculated for an end."[43] He takes possession of his opportunities and his possibilities at that decisive moment of *Bildung*. His choice places him at odds with the expectations of a mercantile usefulness his family once hoped for him. Although Wilhelm is not driven by ethereal notions of perfectibility, his development certainly demands a decisive renunciation of idleness. We might, in this light, understand *Bildung*, whether in Goethe or Humboldt, as a kind of aesthetic counterpart to moral notions of integrity and worthiness. Within the aesthetic sphere, however, self-constitution drives the individual toward particularity, rather than universality. *Bildung* is an autobiographical and deeply personal project. And it must necessarily reject the very idea that we might be happy to rest with ourselves as we find ourselves.

CHAPTER 2

WORK, IDLENESS, AND RESPECT

Among dismissive views of the idea of carefree idleness is that it is a hangover from feudal times. Idleness, in this sense, is a freedom reserved in principle for the few. It resembles little more than the lifestyle of a class of spoiled brats and wastrels whose leisure is parasitic on the labors of others. In the pursuit of their leisure these idlers gain an elevated sense of themselves through indulgent ways of living as contrasting as possible from those which are open to those who need to work for them. They are, in this way, marked out from others not only by their economic advantages and undemocratic power but also by how they act in the world. It is this style of living that Thorstein Veblen captures as "conspicuous leisure," which ostentatiously "connotes . . . a sense of the unworthiness of productive work, and . . . evidence of pecuniary ability to afford a life of idleness."[1] With these worries in front of us, reappraising the case for the value of idleness could involve the unpalatable task of indirectly lending support to the fop or an Oblomov, or of what Bertrand Russell called the "snobbish admiration of useless-ness."[2] Today's general idea of fairness decisively tilts moral judgment—at least in principle—against feudal advantage and the network of values that sustain it.

We should acknowledge that there are some people who, potentially at least, can enjoy the kind of inde-pendence that in the past was once reserved for the few. There does not seem to be widespread desire to stand in the way of these people's unlimited pursuit of leisure if the resources needed for it have been gained through astute career management or perhaps some type of honest luck. Strict egalitarians obviously take a different view. These cases, however, hardly give us access to what is controversially attractive about idle-ness, since they are instances of leisure achieved either following extraordinary and dedicated effort or utter chance. Idleness in this form, in other words, does not really oppose the general order of things.

Not every one of our thoughts about idleness, though, is wrapped up in aristocratic fantasies. There is also that beguiling kind of—what we call—idleness that seems to be part of the daily lives of some commu-nities that we like to believe remain untouched by no-tions of industry and discipline. We have seen Kant's unease with the example offered by the charming but simple people of the South Seas Islands. Why can't we live like them? The desire behind this question is clearly not that we emulate the privileged few or the feckless billionaire. Far from it. It is, in some sense, an appeal to a feature of our humanity that we believe we have lost: living without friction, ambition, visibility, and external demand for productivity beyond what is most basic. Idleness of this sort requires nothing less than elimination of the fundamental mechanics of modern societies: nonessential labor, advantage, competition, admiration of wealth. Kant tried to deal with this supposedly primitive vision of happiness by trumping it with the myth of worthiness. That myth gives us a fine story about human excellence even as it urges painful work. Kant tells us to be serious about ourselves and that satisfaction of a sort will follow. The effectiveness of his position depends on whether we find its complex of principles and arguments strong enough to overwhelm any sense we might have of the desirability of idleness. If we accept Kant's view, then we dismiss that desire as a foolish one. Equally, we might regard the Kantian complex as an alien intrusion that can never really target the appeal of idleness.

A more ingenious case against idleness is made by Hegel. His point of attack is to start with human beings as they are in modern societies and to show, in effect, that it is idleness that is the alien element. His position, as we shall see, presents the proponents of idleness with this difficult objection: namely, that it is a culturally specific fantasy that owes its existence to the very kind of society against which it directs itself. There can be, in effect, no coherent return to naïveté. A great deal of the reason why Hegel believes that return is impossible is not that we have an incorrigible though abstract belief in the value of industry. It goes much deeper than the cognitive level. We gain a sense of freedom in the way we involve ourselves with others in society. Work is a mode of that involvement. We are identified as individuals who contribute to the needs of others, providing those goods and services that are characteristic of the life-world to which we belong. Work therefore allows us to become fully fledged and respected communal beings. Hegel's basic objection, then, is that a desire for idleness is a desire for something of which we are not really capable, given the superior kinds of people modern society has made of us. In contrast with the theory offered by Kant, Hegel does not wave in front of us a picture of what we might be. His account of why we ought to work is a description of what we actually are.

In this chapter, Hegel's radical rejection of idleness will be considered in some detail. I will then turn to Marx, who adopts many of Hegel's ideas about the necessity of work in enabling us to become true social beings. This perspective motivates Marx to confront a number of positions that entertain in various ways idleness as a kind of good. Marx unites with Hegel in thinking that meeting social demands, of certain kinds, is the hallmark of the most developed individuals. These individuals are thought to be uniquely free. For them, the problematic quality of idleness consists effectively in its detachment from a context in which elevating social demands can be placed on us. This means that freedom cannot be found in idleness, but only in the most sublime forms of social exchange. Hegel and Marx attempt to gain ground for this thesis by undermining the intellectual coherence and moral legitimacy of idleness. What they want to give us, instead, is reason to accept that high levels of socially motivated industry and exertion are the means by which true fulfillment can be reached. This amounts to a new justification in theory for what is only sometimes experienced in practice. That is to see social regard, the opinion of others, and recognition as the most fundamental needs. This conception of what we need, however, is partial, gaining some kind of authority, as it tries, by linking itself to ethics and morality. Hegel and Marx are important opponents of the pleasure we may find in withdrawal from the social gaze. The very existence of a desire not to play along with expectations must, they think, be exposed as either a failing on the part of individuals or as a structural deficiency within a community's capacity to provide the circumstances that allow respect to be gained. The material examined in this chapter gives us the opportunity, then, to address the notion that work is fundamental to our self-realization as free beings.

HEGEL'S SELF-PERPETUATING WORKER

Hegel's various thoughts about work might serve to explain the basis of the real difficulty that we can experience in embracing idleness as a way of being for any significant length of time. There is some appeal in the idea of doing nothing in particular, in stepping away from expectations of productivity and admirable usefulness. The unwelcome side of a virtuously industrious life is the unhealthy stressfulness that comes with it. Management consultants mouth unnerving imperatives: "We need to move fast just to stand still," and the like. A moderately productive or balanced life is not really what the world of work wants from us. But even as we know all of that, and would notionally, at least, be happy to subvert it, a kind of inner restlessness speaks against it. When work is not brutal, exploitative, or repetitive, it seems to draw us back. We might think that some happy space between work and idleness could be found. In that space we could meet that restlessness without being consumed by it.

Tolstoy, in fact, finds this very reality in one specific form of life:

Fallen man has retained a love of idleness, but the curse weighs on the race not only because we have to seek our bread in the sweat of our brows, but because our moral nature is such that we cannot be both idle and at ease. An inner voice tells us we are in the wrong if we are idle. If man could find a state in which he felt that though idle he was fulfilling his duty, he would have found one of the conditions of man's primitive blessedness. And such a state of obligatory and irreproachable idleness is the lot of a whole class—the military. The chief attraction of military service has consisted and will consist in this compulsory and irreproachable idleness.[3]

There is, at first, something compelling about this condition. The call of that "inner voice" is met without any real self-sacrifice. The soldiers, placed far from war, earn their keep and indeed can enjoy whatever respect comes with their professions. But the notion of an "inner voice" that disturbs our idleness is complicated. In Tolstoy's words, its origin lies in our moral nature. What, though, is the source of that nature? Hegel explains it as a capacity we gain through the right kind of socialization. There is, however, a question here about the need to be socialized in just that way, or to think of that socialization as moral.

From some perspectives work is not something we should try to outmaneuver, as Tolstoy's soldiers manage to do, by joining some institution of work that will leave us pleasingly underemployed. For many, work offers a very meaningful kind of fulfillment, and idleness is a loss of that meaning. Separation from work can itself be a cause of nagging anxiety. And it is far from unusual for people to fear the prospect of retirement as a permanent cessation of the form of work around which their sense of fulfillment may have been built. Satisfaction for those in "good jobs" can be gained by getting through work that is valued. For these people, idle time, other than recuperative leisure, may be uncomfortable. There is real bite in the self-

accusation that a day has passed with nothing to show
for it: it is time wasted.

Why care, though? Every thoughtful person knows
that nothing we achieve really matters in the end.
What difference does it make that one was or was not
promoted within the ranks of one's profession? Why
does making a name for oneself have such a hold? For
many, pursuit of achievement is just the way we are.
But not all. There is also the view that we are driven to
work by psychological motivations with which we do
not fully identify. We often wish we could metaphori-
cally, to paraphrase Pascal, stay quietly in our rooms.
There is an appreciation that the world as we know it
might come to a chaotic end were we all to do so, but
some element of the withdrawal nonetheless feels attractive. That attraction is usually defeated by the
countervailing compulsion to be active and effective
in the world, active, that is, in ways that go beyond
what is required for basic survival. This may take the
form of an all-consuming pursuit of respect or of
"standing."

In becoming useful in meeting the needs of others—whatever they may be, from health care to en-
tertainment—we move out from our original obscu-
rity and insignificance. A sensible view of this new
standing is to see it as overvalued. It is driven by the
need to make an impression on others, but those others surely do not care as much for our efforts as we do
ourselves. To acknowledge the allure of idleness—of

a simpler, less vigorous life—and to know that there is something approaching emptiness in attempting to make an impression on others are together not powerful enough to prevent us from binding ourselves to our work. Set against that reality, idleness is an insubstantial and passing whim. Hegel's theory supports the countervailing and stronger appeal of work. It effectively justifies the victory of work over a discredited idleness. However, the account he offers does not settle the matter. Instead, it seems only to affirm those most trying features of modern life, features that negatively motivate the appeal of idleness.

From Slavery to Self-Servitude

Hegel's story of how human beings were eventually to become social actors, oriented toward the needs of others, begins with slavery and the conquest of shapeless desire. His famous discussion of the relationship of master and slave offers us an imaginative glimpse into the painful early steps that have led us to the social balance Hegel finds in modern society. A world in which there is a unity of "being-for-another" and "being-for-self" requires some form of reciprocity among individuals.[4] But, according to Hegel, this reciprocity is an achievement. It is found neither in the natural state nor in rudimentary societies. Social formations, he believes, begin with inequality, in which some people are masters and some are slaves. As societies progress, these two forms of life eventually disappear. We become, in a sense, our own masters, driven not by the threats of an outsider, but by our own commands. Work, in Hegel's social sense, replaces enslaved labor. That, at least, is the official narrative of Hegel's theory.

What becomes apparent is that there are features of our original slavery that continue to assert themselves even in what Hegel sees as work in its better forms. In other contexts Hegel makes plausible the idea that part of a sufficient explanation of any given phenomenon will require reference to the conditions that brought that phenomenon about. These conditions recede from view as the phenomenon develops, but they do not disappear. The meaning of any phenomenon lies both in its relation to other phenomena and to its history. Its history comprises its earlier forms as well as the solutions that were found when those forms came—for whatever reason—to seem unsustainable. Modern work is represented by Hegel as, in part, a reconciliation of the extremes of the slave's unfreedom and his master's idleness. It is, however, a reconciliation that tilts toward the greater significance of the unfree, slavelike features of work. The triumph of self-mastery can look, after all, like a process of self-enslavement. The freedom enjoyed by the non-slave—idleness, in effect—is largely eliminated as our social world develops. Whatever vestiges of idleness remain are dealt with by Hegel with several unsecured contentions (as the discussion in the following section will explain).

Hegel's dialectic of master and slave—a chapter of the *Phenomenology of Spirit*—tells us, in a genre all of its own, of social developments that will eventually arrive at the stage where interactions among individuals have the quality of mutual "recognition." Recognition is central to Hegel's idea of the various ways in which modern life has enabled us both to be free, social, and at home among others. We are fulfilled when we are recognized as that which we want to be recognized as: as, among other things, the bearer of rights, a good citizen, a contributor of whatever kind to the social good. This recognition is given by others whose recognition matters to us. They have a standing—recognition of their own—that qualifies them as people whose recognition is worth something within whatever sphere we too wish to be recognized. Recognition, then, exists within webs of reciprocity. The dialectic of master and slave features two notional individuals who are struggling to regain a natural sense of seamless unity with the world. This sense was lost when each first noticed the presence of the other one (their first experiences of another person). By witnessing each other's distinctly human features, each of them came to the realization that they—as human beings—are not simply part of nature. This is the original trauma. The ongoing development of social forms is understood as an effort to restore the peace and freedom lost through that trauma. This restoration is not to be accomplished by returning to nature. Modern life, Hegel believes, achieves that restoration by establishing reasonable social institutions. Reciprocal recognition is enjoyed by those who belong to these institutions. They place us in ethical relations with others and provide us with the only meaningful context in which we can be said to be properly free.

We can step into the dialectic at the point at which, following a life and death struggle for supremacy between Hegel's notional protagonists, the problematic institutions of mastery and of slavery are established. The loser has been placed in servitude. Within this social configuration there is, Hegel holds, one type of agent who has the authority to determine what is true. This is the master. The slave takes his truth from whatever the master declares. In this respect the slave is utterly dependent on the master. The slave is in this position because rather than die he preferred life under these conditions. He is regarded by the master as an "unessential" being.[5] That is, the slave brings nothing of significance to the mental world of the master. One slave is much the same as another, and, by virtue of his status, may not contribute to the business of determining what is right or wrong or true or false. Although the master clearly enjoys the more agreeable of the two forms of life, Hegel suggests that he is nevertheless in a dissatisfying situation. The master is certainly secure as a master, but he is isolated from the world in a number of respects. The most obvious of these is that he does not directly deal with nature, since the slave is set to work on it on his behalf. More deeply, though, the master is isolated because he does not enjoy recognition that would matter to him. That is, there is no other individual of comparable status who can appreciate him positively for what he is. The master does not know that he lacks this recognition, obviously enough, since he has never experienced it. But its absence is somehow perturbing. The slave does perceive the master as a master, but his kind of recognition is worthless. The slave, again, is an unessential consciousness who has no independent view of the world.[6] At best he is coerced into mirroring back the master's own view of himself, but he cannot add any value to that view.

We probably think that the slave's lot is therefore an unqualified misery, a life of fearful obedience and dependence. However, Hegel believes that there are unexpected advantages to being a slave in this specific context. These advantages might be seen only in retrospect in that they are part of the story of how modern social actors came to be. Nevertheless, there is a kind of inversion in the order of ascendancy of the two protagonists, with the slave in some respects enjoying the world more richly than the master can. The slave has no authority in deciding generally how he may spend his time. Yet this subordination opens up the space in which he can at least concentrate on the work tasks that are set for him. Hegel does not have in mind an infernal world of slave drivers, pitilessly counting out every moment of the slave's actions. In this peculiarly

idyllic setting the slave, though institutionally unfree—he is a slave—brings something that is his alone
to the manner in which his set tasks will be performed.
This something is his own individuality: he has a personality, and it comes to be invested in the objects he
must make. This may not seem like a great deal of freedom, but Hegel sees it otherwise. The slave's ability to
invest in the world in this way produces, Hegel claims,
"a truly independent consciousness." The slave "becomes conscious of what he truly is." What he truly is
from our perspective is a slave, but in Hegel's view of
the matter he is now a worker able to make his mark
on nature in accordance with who he is. Through
work this Plautine character establishes a sense of self
that is not reducible to the commands given to him by
the master. The slave does not own himself, but he
possesses himself in a more profound sense than even
the master can manage: "it is precisely in his work
wherein he seemed to have only an alienated existence
that he acquires a mind of his own."[7]

However, it is not initiative or an inner yearning
for self-realization that carries the slave to this new
level of consciousness of what he can do. A condition of acquiring a "mind" is "fear." After all, the slave's
discipline comes about only because the master has
total power over him. This significant moment of development will not occur unless the slave fully appre-
ciates the existential importance of setting aside his
own passing desires and placing himself entirely at
ready service to the master. Work, for this reason, is

"fleetingness staved off." It imposes an order on the slave's desires. The transition to some sense of independence comes about against the grain of what we might expect of servitude. What allows it to happen is that the slave experiences "the two moments of fear and service." He is driven to work by these two forces, but without them he would never have sought to attempt to express himself in nature. The violence and vulnerability of his situation lead him to discover skillful work: "universal formative activity." Without "absolute fear"—fear that intimates to the slave his sheer mortality—and instead "only some lesser dread," the slave will approach work with "an empty self-centred attitude," mired in his own "self-will" and a "mind of" his "own."[8] This recalcitrance will deprive him of a developmental opportunity as well as the satisfaction of giving form—his own—to nature. That opportunity is one from which modern ideas of work and usefulness have grown.

The master does not have tasks. He is an idler, moved solely and without planning by those fleeting desires that are the basis of his commands to the obedient slave. As a creature of desire he is not, in contrast with the slave, a person. The slave requires discipline in order to work as instructed. This discipline brings about, for Hegel, a stable self. The master is an exemplar of idleness, and he, by contrast, remains unrealized as a social actor. That, for Hegel, is the master's deficit. Freedom in Hegel's sense therefore does not even begin to apply to him. He has no identity and can never have one precisely because of his idleness: desire cannot give rise to the kind of enduring self that can invest itself in objects. The master is therefore unable to make himself public. What we have seen of the slave, by contrast, is an inchoate yet philosophically discernible sense of freedom that is attached to his work, that is, to his public existence. He can objectify himself in nature. Endurance of the slave's kind is brought about through strict regulation of unruly desire.

Why, though, outside the primal conditions in which Hegel's dialectic is set, does the discipline that emerged in the slave persist? What is the source of that fear that brings about the attitude of service alongside the wish to express ourselves in objects and to make ourselves public? The external master has, we might conjecture, evolved into self-mastery. But mastery that we do not fear, if we follow Hegel's line of thought, would have no meaning. Perhaps the fear we experience now, through our own hand, is that distinctive anxiety that seems to accompany our need to be recognized in our work. We sense the possibility that everything we might ever make of ourselves could be lost were we to fall outside the world of work. We succeed when we do what others admire. A certain kind of death is faced by those who fail to meet the expectations of their professions. Self-mastery, if this is what it amounts to, is cruel. And it is paradoxical too. The freedom that seems to be gained by becoming one's own master is tied to the opinion of others of how well we have used our own powers. The disposition of the slave is there after all. The concepts of self-mastery and self-enslavement are two ways of defining the very same phenomenon: service with fear. All of this is a consequence of Hegel's unique genealogy of the modern social actor. After all, that reconstruction emphasizes its servile lineage. The master's idleness is destined never to develop: it is hopeless, chaotic desire, with no discipline, no orientation toward others, either for their approval or to meet their needs. This disposition cannot be improved, and it simply falls away from the story of what we have become. As Alexandre Kojève rightly puts it, "If idle Mastery is an impasse, laborious Slavery, in contrast, is the source of all human, social, historical progress. History is the history of the working Slave."[9] As we shall see, Hegel deepens this history through his account of the exchanges within modern societies. All talk of masters, slaves, and fear is dropped. Yet the basic dispositions that were graphically set out in the dialectic remain.

Inside the System of Needs

In the *Philosophy of Right*, Hegel clarifies and elaborates on some of the elements of work and service that we have seen in the dialectic of master and slave. A ready willingness to be useful to society is among the attributes he finds in the properly formed modern individual. He maintains that we make ourselves useful by working. Work in the sense that interests Hegel is not a capacity found in a state of nature. It is gained only through education and socialization. By usefulness Hegel does not mean that we ought to become instruments for others, that is to say, useful in the way that tools are. Rather, work allows us both to serve the needs of others and to realize ourselves as complex and free communal beings.

These ideas are set out in the third part of his *Philosophy of Right*. The first part of that book deals with "abstract right," the formal freedom permitted by the law. "Morality"—the second part—considers the kind of freedom that is implied by theories that rest freedom on the individual power of conscience. Hegel judges both of these perspectives to be no more than partial views of freedom. What they cannot capture is a picture of the actions of individuals understood as free responses to and enactments of the norms of the community as a whole. And this is because those perspectives do not realize that a fundamental precondition of freedom is individual social formation. In different ways, they set the individual against the outer world. As Hegel explains in "Ethical Life"— the third and culminating part of the *Philosophy of Right*—it is through that formation that we become social actors, engaging freely in activities that express some aspect of what we truly take ourselves to be. The objectivity of what we take ourselves to be is established through patterns of social interaction that we have seen Hegel define in the dialectic of master and slave as "recognition." In considering work as something that takes place within "ethical life," Hegel sits far from the tragic view that work is little more than an imposition or merely a natural necessity. Rather, it is for him a basic dimension of properly formed social actors. We can see from this brief characterization of Hegel's theory that the very idea of idleness as a form of freedom is cut off from the beginning. Since work and the possession of a recognizable place in society are the hallmarks of our freedom, idleness would seem to be a kind of violation of what modern life has made of us.

Hegel places work within a sphere of "ethical life" he calls the "system of needs." This system, he tells us, involves the "mediation of *need* and the satisfaction of the *individual* through the work and satisfaction of the need of *all the others*."[10] One of his principal claims is that work places us in a social world. The notional purely private space of the self would remain isolated and dissatisfyingly underdeveloped if it did not invest itself through work in "external things." How we invest and what we invest in are in some respects personal choices. But the "satisfaction" we manage to achieve has a strict relationship with the degree to which those choices relate to the needs of others (those others are not, in this context, our masters). Hegel, then, is not offering a general story of the basic dynamic of a market economy: the invisible hand that guides production in some putatively efficient way. He does, in fact, agree with that classical view. For him, however, we must primarily consider the deeper truth that underpins the system of needs, namely, that it is an important feature of what it means to be a modern social being. Hegel accents above all the interdependent relations that form the system. These relations are not like contracts that connect one party to another for a specific purpose and time. They are, rather, "conciliatory" and in that sense what Hegel thinks of as "ethical": they bring us together on grounds that surpass shared self-interest.[11]

The meaning of this extra ingredient of ethics is elusive in this context. An ethical quality is not found in any feeling we might have about the needs of others (other than the restricted sphere of family and friendship): Hegel does not think the system operates through conscious acts of altruism or a love of community and its values. Nor do we attempt to express any kind of moral principle or demonstrate virtue when performing effectively within the system. Hegel, however, places a great deal of weight on the supposed ethical quality of the system. It is ethical from some point of view other than that of the people who make it happen. When Hegel explains why we are motivated to make some goods rather than others, the explanations work perfectly well as accounts of rational economic choices, yet he insists that they have an ethical character. Equally, his use of "recognition" in this context appears to have an elevated quality that cannot be found in the description of what actually happens among producers and consumers. He claims that the relationship between producer and consumer has "the quality of being recognized."[12] The producer recognizes the value of what is needed—being wanted by someone makes it valuable—and the consumer recognizes the producer's role as someone who can help fulfill those needs. Hegel uses the discovered ethical quality of these transactions to justify a system of work. The "moral nature" that Tolstoy saw as the basis of our compulsion to set aside idleness is now explained as role playing within an "ethical" system of needs and exchange.

Social needs are clearly complex, having little to do with biological necessities. What we think we need is, Hegel claims, determined by "opinion."[13] We freely subject ourselves to the assessment of others who will view us according to prevailing standards of "taste and utility." Meeting those standards enables us "to fit in with other people."[14] This, among other things, is considered by Hegel to be a fundamental need of social beings. He does not think that "fitting in" is to be found in a state of nature. Civilized people are responsive to the regard of others and motivated to achieve what others esteem. In that way, our actions "transcend" our animality.[15] This line of thinking seems to validate Veblen's jaundiced epithet, "conspicuous." But for Hegel, being visible to others and approved by them in this way is a positive thing. Rather than experiencing "opinion" as a source of persecution, we must, he holds, see it as a "liberation." The argument he supplies in behalf of this surprising claim runs to the effect that opinion is a norm we social beings give to ourselves. The needs that arise through opinion express, as he puts it, "man's relation to *his own opinion.*"[16] We might think it hostile to realizing ourselves in our own idiosyncratic ways to understand and approve of ourselves in terms of opinions that precede us. There could be satisfaction in esteem and in being respected for accomplishments. But there may also be shame and inhibition where we cannot see beyond what is measured by the opinions of others. Oscar Wilde, who had much reason to despise convention, captures the problem: "Most people are other people. Their thoughts are someone else's opinions, their lives a mimicry, their passions a quotation" (*De profundis*). Hegel, however, regards it as an aspect of our freedom that we wish to satisfy opinion. If opinion is experienced as a constraint it is, in effect, a positively and humanly self-legislated one.

According to this thought, those whose needs are purely natural do not experience this liberation. There is instead only "savagery and unfreedom" in the state of nature.[17] The contrast Hegel draws is stark: liberating opinion or brute simplicity. He withholds comment on the content of any of these means of liberation, that is, of what "opinion" might lead us to need or act upon. It is quite compatible with his view of opinion-based need that the acquisition of prestigious consumer goods would be liberation. Hegel pillories Diogenes for his doomed attempt to react against the luxuries—the objectionable opinion, we might say—

of Athens. Precisely as a targeted rebellion, Hegel maintains, Diogenes was "determined" by "the opinion against which his entire way of life reacted."[18] This response to Diogenes has wider implications in that it supports Hegel's idea that "opinion" is ineluctable for socialized beings: either they willingly acquiesce with this norm, as most generally do, or they resist in a way that confirms how deeply they have internalized this norm. They define themselves as individuals who resist, but resistance has a content, and rebels like Diogenes are not the authors of that content. Hegel's assessment of Diogenes's "unprepossessing" rebellion is harsh.[19] It is possible that he is disgusted by Diogenes's charmless public actions. If, as is more likely, the assessment sits on philosophical grounds, then Hegel is making a strike against any efforts to promote life freed from "opinion." While the style of criticism Hegel brings against Diogenes does not explicitly recommend conformism, it hardly permits that alternative forms of behavior might be understood to have positive grounds of their own. This is a significant line of thought with clear implications for the claims of freedom we might associate with idleness, among other things. The idler's rebellion, according to the pattern of this type of argument, does nothing more than confirm the significance of usefulness. The idler is an unhappy or ill-fitting member of society whose dreams of escape from usefulness are baseless. They have no positive grounds.

This baselessness comes into sharp focus when we appreciate what Hegel sees as the reach of education. He maintains that we gain the capacity to serve the system of needs—to be a worker—through what he calls "practical education." He makes a hard distinction between practical and theoretical education. The latter involves, in effect, acquiring a capacity to use concepts. The former, though, seems to mean developing a very specific kind of disposition. He writes: "*Practical education* through work consists in the self-perpetuating need and *habit of being occupied* in one way or another, in the *limitation of one's activity* to suit both the nature of the material in question and, in particular, the arbitrary will of others, and in a habit, acquired through this discipline, of *objective activity* and *universally applicable skills*."[20] (Elsewhere Hegel explains this "arbitrary will of others" as having negative consequences for the freedom of those who are subject to that arbitrariness.)[21]

That disposition has, we see, an array of facets: a work ethic or habit, production, a specific skill, responsiveness to the needs of others. All these features combine to make a useful worker.[22] An example of humanity that has never had the advantages of education for serviceability is the barbarian. This exotic human being, Hegel thinks, is not to be admired. He may well have in mind a non-European from one of those parts of the known world then gaining closer attention in the West thanks to exploration and the

attendant search for commercial and colonial opportunities. Industrious Europeans, as Sarah Jordan puts
it, often saw the lives of these outsiders as "a display of
disgusting indolence, rather than, for instance, a pastoral enjoyment of Edenic leisure."[23] Hegel likewise
regards the barbarian as a lowly type of being. The barbarian leads a "lazy" life of "dull and solitary brood-
ing" without that commendable "need and habit of
being occupied."[24] Clearly, this sort of human falls
short of the characteristics of the properly socialized
individual, though it is not so obvious why Hegel
takes this form of life to be solitary. That view is likely
to be a convenience to his system: civilization involves
recognition and mutuality, barbarism its absence.
What better way to explain that absence than by de-
claring that the savage does not have social relations?
(There is perhaps a hint that what Hegel sees as a
modern underclass—the "rabble"—can enjoy primitive social relations, though they are certainly to be
feared as sinister, anarchic, and unreasonable idlers.)[25]
As a consequence of that absence, the barbarian is also
deprived of—some might think saved from—both
the "liberating" pressure of "opinion" and "the arbitrary will of others." There is in any case no kudos—
nothing worthy of recognition—in attending to basic
animal needs. The barbarian may be perfectly self-
sufficient—though this is not acknowledged—but
there is no value in his "immediate" work: work that
is undertaken by an individual merely to satisfy the
unplanned demands of present circumstances. It no

doubt requires some effort, but it is not, in Hegel's special sense, "ethical." Hegel's conception of the barbarian is hard to entertain, generating as it does animalistic images of human beings who exist outside multilayered civilizations. Nevertheless, this conception has a significant role to play in outlawing any kind of Diogenean rebellion against usefulness: it turns that rebellion into an absurd and self-defeating desire for dullness, solitariness, and crude need.

Hegel has decided that socialization of the ethical kind is found only in highly organized, long established, and large human settlements. Socialized beings are not lazy or idle: practical education is supposed to see to that. This education allows the system to prosper and everyone in it to achieve some type of recognition along with their other nonmaterial needs.[26] If we try, though, to take the perspective of the barbarian, Hegel's idea of superior humanity may seem perverse. Since the preservation of the barbarian's life is already secured by doing no more work than is necessary, how could he be persuaded that a "need and habit of being occupied" represents a step up from his form of life? Indeed, arguably that "need and habit" sometimes produces in us all an unwelcome agitation that disrupts ease and leisure. If part of the appeal of idleness lies in its image of escape from "opinion," then we should want to reject Hegel's assessment of the barbarian. The barbarian, it appears, has precisely those freedoms that we rarely enjoy: he works only when required to sustain himself, is not restless, does not undertake long-term projects that effectively hold him captive, and, again, he does not suffer the intrusions of what others think he ought to do or be.

We may indulge our imaginations in this fantasy, but, from the Hegelian point of view, we cannot defend it as a life for us. That would involve us in projecting ourselves into a space that is completely at odds with what we—the beings doing the imagining—actually are. Our fantasy of release into barbarian idleness is as ill-founded as the desire of Diogenes—a man of the city—for a simplicity that stands in judgment on luxurious Athens. We are creatures of the "system of needs." To think hostilely of the world from which we have come assumes the impossible: that we could return, by way of imitation, to the natural immediacy of the barbarian. This is a decisive line of thought that attempts to choke off rational justification for quite different ways of living. The naïveté of the barbarian can only be imitated, but it cannot be true for us.

Experience probably tells many of us that the social formation that gives work its meaning is not as deep or as compelling as Hegel believes. Work is not necessarily embraced, even when it is available, as a sphere of self-realization. Roland Paulsen's study of the workplace gives firmer evidence to these thoughts. His research suggests that where workers are not monitored or subject to extreme workloads, they may instead turn to idleness rather than show initiative to devise absorbing new tasks. Employees—it may not be quite right to call them workers—can actually find value in their situation through their idle activities, be they socializing with colleagues during work hours or "webloafing." But this value owes nothing to the work process and its supposed glories. "Empty laborers," as Paulsen labels them, generally occupy positions with at least a good level of social status and that possess the very kinds of conditions that progressive social theorists favor: the skill quality of the work they are expected to undertake is high, remuneration is no less than average, they are secure in their employment, work in physical safety, are not obliged to be available at unusual hours. Yet, they—we—idle in spite of the conditions in which flourishing, satisfaction, and contribution to the common good all lie notionally within easy reach. There is a sense, then, that individuals find in contexts of empty labor a way beyond the desire formation they are supposed to have, linked as it is with work and self-elevation.[27]

Hegel, as we have seen, claims that we cannot escape our socialization. He also expects us to balk at the life of idleness he sees in the wretched barbarian. But the socialization thesis as applied to the Diogenean rebel does no more than insist on its own truth. And that we should respond to the life of the barbarian as Hegel would want is far from certain when the alternative to that life is inextricably attached to that painful history captured in the earlier story of the master and slave. If we disavow idleness, it is to resume a life of self-mastery and self-enslavement. Hegel is obviously right about the grip this life has for many.

But what he does not acknowledge are the burdens it brings with it: a fearful anxiety to succeed in terms that are not necessarily our own. Idleness is, in this context, the name for everything that stands opposed to the way of life the modern world has given us. And until that world is no longer the source of anxiety, idleness is likely to have its appeal. Marx's ideas about work, as we shall now see, might be understood as the attempt to reform the world in which idleness persists as an attractive alternative to the system Hegel celebrates.

MARX AND THE ASOCIAL IDLER

Marx adopts many of the ideas found in Hegel's theory of work. Unlike Hegel, he does not attempt to justify the institution of work as it is found in the contemporary world. Rather, he offers a vision of work under what he regards as circumstances that society has generally yet to create for itself. For Hegel, liberating work is a reality, but Marx can view it only as an aspiration. This basic commitment provides him with a distinctive perspective from which to assess the appeal of idleness. Whereas Hegel argues that our social formation rules out laziness and idleness as viable ways of life, Marx, by contrast, sees idleness as an understandable attraction—analogous perhaps to the attractions of religion—in a world in which work practices involve a violence to ourselves.

What Marx takes to be the character of fulfilling work differs from what we find in Hegel. Marx believes that workers will, in the ideal situation, be, in effect, morally motivated. Hegel had characterized the system itself—not its agents—as an ethical one. Marx's distinctive assessment of idleness is a consequence of this moral standpoint. He sees it as egoism. Idleness involves a disregard for a community of others to whom we owe sentimental duties of care. But it is also a disregard for our obligation to ourselves individually to increase our own powers and capacities. Marx tends to conceive this behavior in terms of laziness—*Faulheit*—perhaps suggesting that inaction is not innocent: it is rather a lack of willingness to do what one knows one should. It may be that circumstances explain why many are drawn to idleness, but that does not alter its selfish quality. The presence of idleness reveals something about the conditions that generate selfishness. Marx places an image of developed humanity before us and judges any impediment to that image in principled terms. The ideal to be reached in Marx's case requires intersubjective action. Hence the worry about any behavior or way of life— idleness par excellence—that would place us outside the space of intersubjective exchanges. These views are found across writings from Marx's early period and a little beyond.[28]

A central difficulty of Marx's position lies in its effort to justify its condemnation of laziness or idleness among those who do not belong to the exploiting classes. This condemnation owes nothing to the traditional worry about the latent decadence of the idler. Rather, laziness is an opportunity lost, since it prevents us from realizing ourselves among a community of sympathetic companions. As we shall go on to explore, work as Marx conceives it in its ideal form is, among other things, a pleasurable moral enterprise, guided by a conscious interest in the welfare and happiness of others. Any call for leisurely idleness or a defense of lazy reluctance is based on a misunderstanding of what work could be, wrongly predicated on what is merely today's miserable reality. That is a reality in which there is no community and no fulfillment in collective action. Idleness is, in this regard, a symptom of alienation even as it offers itself as an escape from alienating conditions. As contributions to constructive social criticism, Marx's claims depend, then, first, on a moral point of view (that work is to be motivated by concern for others) and, second, on a specific image of what shape life would take under the best circumstances (the pursuit of self-realization). Because these claims are connected with values and ideals that are widely shared, they may seem to be relatively uncontroversial. However, the practical implications are more complicated: idleness is to be replaced by work in a superior form. To even begin to succeed, Marx's claims should convince those who find freedom in idleness that its advantages—pleasure, happiness, peace—can be superseded at least without loss. Only then might surrendering any continuing com-

mitment to idleness in favor of a life of work come to
seem tenable.

Idleness as Asociality

Marx adopts Hegel's thesis that work prompted by immediate needs has no social presence. Things made in
this context satisfy the maker alone. He writes: "For
man himself—in a savage, barbaric condition—therefore, the amount of his production is determined by
the *extent* of his immediate need, the content of which
is *directly* the object produced."[29] But Marx's theory,
unlike Hegel's, is geared famously toward understanding the destructive tendencies of work under the conditions of capitalism. This interest explains his quite
un-Hegelian view that there are intrinsic similarities
between barbarian selfishness and the modern version
of work. At one level his point is quite mistaken: the
barbarian, after all, does not live in an alienated condition, and furthermore he has the opportunity to idle.
The two forms of life, however, are alike in one key
respect. They are devoid of an expressive dimension.
The savage, as Hegel had established, works out of immediacy with no thought of making an impression on
others or imprinting himself on the world. His work
is expressionless in that specific sense: it says nothing
about him. Brutalized workers can think only of survival. And what they produce is made following a plan
over which they have no influence. They are precluded

from expressing themselves in the objects they make. Like the savage, they cannot become public, in the sense that Hegel developed. Their products enter a market to meet the needs of others among whom sodality is not even imaginable. The barbarian is socially invisible, and in some sense modern workers are too in that their personalities may not enter the things they make. In these senses, then, modern work reverts to the empty, expressionless efforts of the barbarian.

Marx sets out an ideal situation in which work would be free of those barbaric tendencies: "In my *production* I would have objectified my *individuality, its specific character*, and therefore enjoyed not only an individual *manifestation of my life* during the activity, but also when looking at the object I would have the individual pleasure of knowing my personality to be *objective, visible to the senses* and hence a power *beyond all doubt*."[30] This passage brings the various parts of Hegel's system of needs to mind: there is the sense of gaining a standing by satisfying the needs of others. But Marx's account of production has the additional ambition of invoking the *affective* dimension of meeting the needs of others: it has something to do with caring about them. He writes: "In your enjoyment or use of my product I would have the *direct* enjoyment both of being conscious of having satisfied a *human* need by my work, that is, of having objectified *man's* essential nature, and of having thus created an object corresponding to the need of another *man's* essential nature."[31] It is in this way that Marx commits his theory to something that looks like the traditional quality of altruism. The mutual regard between producer and consumer goes further than the implicit exchanges of Hegel's notion of recognition. Hegel's system of relations allows—even as he labels it "ethical"—that we might care little for each other and still be fully formed socially productive agents. Marx maintains that we cannot *truly* realize ourselves without productivity.

It is hardly surprising, then, that he is a particularly keen critic of positions that either favor idleness or unwittingly open up social spaces within which idleness might be permissible. One of the most pointed criticisms of the former appears in his and Engels's *German Ideology* in response to an attack by Max Stirner on communism.[32] Stirner had offered a characteristically narrow and combative defense of the sovereign individual against what he saw as the leveling values of a communist society. Marx and Engels quote a long passage from Stirner in which he claims that the very idea of "true well-being" bears the hallmarks of "the tyranny of religion."[33] It is proposed, he thinks, as a "truth" that each of us must accept regardless of whether we are inclined to it. He believes that the communists regard a decent society as one in which "true well-being" includes "honestly earned enjoyment." Enjoyment, in other words, is allegedly socially acceptable once a certain amount of virtuous labor has been completed. But this, he fears, allows no space for those who would prefer a life of "enjoyable idleness" or laziness (*Faulheit*).[34] Stirner builds his case on the distasteful example of "rentiers" (inciting in response something close to a Philippic) whose "enjoyable idleness" is, he laments, threatened by the tyranny of communist universals. Marx and Engels clarify that communism—their version at least—is not in the business of changing the world merely to bring about the possibility of "honestly earned enjoyment." Enjoyment in this form is, they think, nothing but a lower-middle-class conceit. And so too is the idea of "enjoyable idleness" (a taunt that would no doubt have been applied to John Dewey's paradigm "of a truly democratic society, a society in which all share in useful service and all enjoy a worthy leisure.")[35] This shows, they contend, that Stirner cannot think beyond the social relations that form his personal world. The example he uses to undermine communist universalism fails, their argument goes, because Stirner "imagines that for these individuals there can exist no other 'well-being' than that which is determined by their position as rentiers."[36] The conceptual bareness of Stirner's philosophy prevents it from seeing this: a one-dimensional libertarianism is committed to denying that class relations mark our choices.

Marx and Engels's reply to Stirner is hardly decisive in that it hinges on the reassertion of the idea that there is a higher well-being that is without class interest. And Stirner has, in any case, derided the very idea as religious. Stirner's confrontational example prompts the question of whether idleness ultimately belongs to a select social group. He appears to have in mind the kind of idleness that goes with exploitative social arrangements. But this, as we have seen, is only one version of the phenomenon. Interestingly, Marx and Engels do not themselves seem able to look beyond that version. They offer us the limited choice between Stirner's ill-founded idea of "enjoyable idleness" or, as we shall see, a form of pleasure that can come only from work and never from idleness. "Honestly earned leisure" is a concept belonging to a world where approved recreation is among the rewards for admirable toil. But that is a world where work is a painful experience. Marx and Engels maintain that the concept of "honestly earned leisure" is built on the contemporary "opposition between work and enjoyment."[37] This opposition will disappear in the new society they envision. What the revolutionary position aims to do is to abolish simultaneously miserable and socially useless work—work that fulfills neither the worker nor the producer—and the equally useless escapist notions it generates.

Stirner's defense of idleness may be an obvious target for Marx's social criticism. But Marx seems equally troubled by theories—no matter how progressive their intent—that tolerate any level of idleness. In the *Poverty of Philosophy*, he quotes and criticizes at length John Francis Bray's well-meaning proposals for a transition toward a perfectly equitable socialist society. The capacity to function within a socialist society, Bray holds, would require a change of mentality from that which exists under capitalism. The transition from today's norms to those of an egalitarian settlement cannot, though, be made in one step. A strictly regulated system, free of the usual iniquities of capitalism, would be a vital intermediate phase prior to a spontaneously lived socialism. Bray's transitional system precludes the exploitation of labor, inflation of the value of goods, and competition among workers for wages. Individual workers could freely choose to work as much or as little as they preferred, each one "dependent on his own exertions" (quoted by Marx).[38] Marx claims, though, that the rigidity of this system produces an incentive to idleness or laziness. The system is based purely on calculations of fair exchanges of labor—your labor for mine—or of equivalences in products, each product being valued by how much labor is required to complete it. But why is "idleness" perceived as an index of theoretical defect?

Implicit in Marx's criticisms of Bray is his assumption that there is no incentive to do more than the minimum in situations in which work has not become social. The social situation is one where there is an affectionate interest in what we can do for each other while at the same time enjoying the self-realization that comes from crafting things. The consumer's delight in what the producer can offer gives production one dimension of its purpose (alongside the space it provides for self-realization through the development of creative skills and capacities). Social production has none of that coldness found in fair exchange or exact equivalences. Because they are not economically motivated, decisions about work and how we are to produce transcend calculation.

And this brings us back to Marx's comments on Bray. Bray's model might be free of the possibility of exploitative capital and exaggerated value, but it lacks the motivational dimension of labor as Marx conceives it. As a consequence, the worker simply reckons what amount of work is to be undertaken, with the moral hazard, Marx seems to say, of concluding the less work the better. Marx explores Bray's theory through an example: "Let us suppose Peter has 12 hours' labour before him, and Paul only six. Peter will consequently have six hours' labour left over. What will he do with these six hours' labour?"[39] This question would hardly arise in a community where work has an intuitive connection with personal happiness and sociability. Hence, the options put forward by Marx in answer to his own question assume that work avoidance, and therefore a wholly unnecessary if not unacceptable idleness, follows where the right social sense is absent. Marx suggests that "Peter" will either work his extra six hours, though he will have done so for nothing in exchange. Or he will more rationally forgo those six useless hours and "will remain idle for another six hours to get even," in that he will have no surplus that he cannot exchange.[40] Equally, he might try to offload these extra hours, but the recipient would then face the same options. Anyone who acquires extra hours that they cannot reasonably be expected to use, according to Marx, has earned merely hours of leisure. This places the surplus holder in a position—evidently a terrible one—in which he his "forced to play the loafer [*Faulenzer*]."[41] By speaking of "force"—he uses the verb *zwingen*—Marx suggests that there is a kind of unwelcome coercion or compulsion in being made idle in this way. It is not easy to see why he believes this when he also acknowledges that work in that context is itself a dreadful experience: "this society would have to find in idleness [*Faulheit*] its highest bliss, and to look upon labour as a heavy shackle from which it must break free at all costs."[42] From the point of view of that society, "Paul," it seems, is in the better position. Right from the beginning he has little work to do. This society would, though, have its own competitive pressures: the "competition" to be as idle and lazy as possible. Marx takes this to be a situation that speaks against itself. He does not imagine that this outbreak of idleness might lead to social benefits. And that is because he is committed to investing work with the power to give humanity forms of freedom and happiness we usually pursue in other spheres.

A more positive view of the world opened up by Bray's principles is not hard to reach. We could envisage a greater level of sociability and fellowship among people who are protected from societally generated disparities. A community of idlers, or at least part-time workers, could find among themselves opportunities for affective experiences that contrast with the rather tiring type Marx builds into his ideal model of work. Perhaps these are the conditions enjoyed by Tolstoy's soldiers. Work would continue to be a necessary evil, but its place in our lives would be significantly reduced, and not only in terms of time consumed. More important, it would not be seen as the place in which to make something of oneself or to gain a good name according to the judgment of others. We would not be dragged from rest by the nagging feelings of underachievement or of dereliction of duty. Happiness and fulfillment, if available at all, would be sought elsewhere. None of this is in line with Marx's theory. Where idleness is a reasonable preference to work, he thinks, social progress has been compromised.

Marx, then, insists on the preeminence of work in giving meaning to our individual and collective existences. In the *Outlines of the Critique of Political Economy*—the so-called *Grundrisse*—he tackles the prejudice, as he sees it, that work must be displeasurable and a kind of sacrifice of what we really prefer to do. He notes the implicit acceptance by Adam Smith and others of the biblical curse: "In the sweat of thy brow shalt thou labor!" This somber perspective entails that work is an impediment to tranquillity, "liberty," and "happiness." But Smith fails to see that the effort that work requires is of value: it is how "self-realisation" is gained. Certainly, existing versions of work mostly preclude any positive benefit to the worker's development. It would, however, be a mistake to imagine that the effort of work is always a wretched experience. If part of what work involves is effort, then effort itself will form part of ideal work too. When self-realization is possible, industry can become "attractive," but not for Marx in the trivial forms of "fun" or "amusement." On the contrary, the kind of work that can allow us to express our freedom, Marx argues, is "also the most damnably difficult, demanding the most intensive effort."[43] In this way, the effort of work is the very opposite of abject self-sacrifice. Conventional work demands, as Marx elsewhere notes, cruel self-denial. He writes that the worker "does not affirm himself but denies himself" as he "mortifies his body," injuring his capacity for a discriminating, sensuous relationship with things.[44] The discipline of the workplace makes the need for this self-denial clear to the worker. But there is a good kind of self-sacrifice, the elimination of something that ought to have no part in our lives: "What appears as a sacrifice of rest may also be called a sacrifice of idleness [*Faulheit*], of unfreedom, of unhappiness, i.e. the negation of a negative condition," through which we move toward the possibility of "positive, creative activity."[45]

Marx, as we have seen, does not come to his condemnation of idleness by way of the work ethic or a fear of human degeneracy. Its moralism, nevertheless, is in plain evidence. The measure of the "good" is the welfare of the human community. An ideal community just so happens to be the space within which individual human flourishing alone is possible: individual and society as a whole are therefore perfectly in harmony. The appeal of idleness is the call of selfishness. Marx's argument will be a powerful one to those who can happily imagine the prospect of a life of work where there is virtuous exertion and blameless exhaustion. There can be for them no utopia of idleness. Edenic ease is superseded by a self among others who find pleasure in industry. Many might share this particular part of Marx's vision of a better world. To others its hold may be weaker. There is promise in his idea that hard work could become a pleasure, were it like creative work. But constant work of this order of intensity would hardly be universally desirable as the norm. Just as Hegel's world of "recognition" and "opinion" imposes a restless need to work, Marx wants to drive us by persuading us that visible communal enjoyment of our powers is the only true pleasure. Marx, though, must deny for the sake of his theory that there is pleasure in retreat too. He attempts to bring this pleasure into disrepute by aligning it with the vices of a world distorted by capitalism. Experience freed from that distortion awaits us in a new future. Idleness is the enemy of that future. The idler, however, can hardly be alone in wondering whether it is wise to surrender the lesser goods of rest and happiness, among others, in the name of the exertions of work that a speculative notion of higher sociability demands of us.

CHAPTER 3

THE CHALLENGES OF BOREDOM

A prevalent worry about idleness is that it quickly leads to boredom. The idea of acting without end or commitment for any sustained period has, according to this thought, only notional appeal. Experience teaches us that aimless laziness inevitably becomes unsettling. Kant tries to explain this puzzling aspect of our desire for a kind of living that is in reality a source of discomfort. He thinks of the boredom that idleness causes as "a highly contrary feeling" in that it comes about because of our "natural inclination toward ease." Our partiality for "vegetating aimlessly," as he puts it, turns out, however, to be excessively onerous because of the boredom it soon places on us. Ultimately we find ways of passing the time that allow us to escape from boredom, but then we are no longer really idle. In this way we "deceive" our misguided "inclination" for "idle rest."[1] We can tell ourselves that we want nothing but idleness, yet we will tend to take on tasks—often trivial ones—that are not quite in line with the ideal of idleness. Idleness and lazy indifference to the course of our days cannot withstand the competing and stronger urge to throw ourselves into waiting tasks or perhaps to undertake new ones. This experience of being bored when we are without engrossing activities is so often reported that one might assume that it relates to a timeless fact about human psychology.

This near amalgamation of boredom with idleness is not, though, as straightforward as it might appear. It involves, after all, different concepts, with boredom picking out a psychological or emotional state and idleness a form of behavior. Furthermore, boredom is not a necessary consequence of idleness. The various condemnations of idleness—the philosophical worry about its indifference to self-constitution and autonomy, in particular—are based on the apparently troubling yet real possibility that some people at least are perfectly capable of indulging in idleness without being bothered by boredom. None of this is to say, though, that the boredom complaint against idleness is a fabrication. Indeed, it is more solidly grounded than the high-minded criticisms of idleness made by the philosophers we have considered so far. That complaint seems to capture a common experience. Teasing out the basis of that experience is among the main objectives of this chapter. A difficulty in pursuing this specific objective is that the boredom-idleness connection may look like a pearl of everyday wisdom, but it is seldom the topic of any theory, notwithstanding the enormous amount of literature dedicated to the theme of boredom across a number of academic disciplines. The one outstanding philosophical effort to make sense of and effectively explain the apparent inevitability of that connection is found in Schopenhauer's complex and wide-ranging account of what he takes to be the human condition. A considerable portion of this chapter will examine that account.

Schopenhauer holds that it is the deliberate suppression of boredom that leads us to act with intentional ends. That action gives relief through temporary contentment. He offers us a theory of boredom that lays out in the starkest way the dread of idleness that stems from our general aversion to boredom. His forcefully expressed perspective turns on a conflation of a variety of quite different conditions that are thought of as boring and as idle. We shall see too the dependence of that perspective on a very particular view of satisfying human action. There is no assumption here that the exposure of Schopenhauer's commitments ought to lead to any change in our experience of boredom and idleness. What the critical engagement with his ideas should allow, though, is a deeper appreciation of the social basis of an experience that is often understood to be rooted in essential human nature. It might even lead us to think further about boredom as a historical phenomenon, "an invention," as Patricia Spacks puts it, "that became both useful and necessary only at a relatively recent historical moment."[2] Boredom may not, then, be a basic biologically determined emotion, after all, but a historically contextualized process of human self-understanding. That is, it is a concept that has a history that is inseparable from the efforts of human beings to make sense of their experiences. Among the experiences of the modern world are those underpinned by the values of industry and endless personal self-advancement. Perhaps it is those values that instill the very restlessness that disrupts idleness.

We need to look too to the question of gender in the idleness-boredom connection. Some philosophers have tried to convince us that women are spared from the struggle against boring idleness. The motivation that drives this strange claim is in one respect all too obvious and dismally familiar. And it is tempting for that reason to conclude that it merits no consideration. When, though, in responding to the exemption claim, we examine Beauvoir's notion of "the idle woman," the most difficult challenge to the defense of idleness emerges. Beauvoir reveals one context in which idleness stands in tension with freedom. That context is the institution of marriage, of a certain type, where idleness essentially imposes painful limitations on the capacity of women to act toward rewarding ends. What is experienced is not the freedom of idleness but boredom.

Before attending to the main work of this chapter, it should help to have some prior sense of what is generally identified as boredom, since confusion of its various senses often leads to unusual claims about its effects and implications. We can begin with the question of how many forms boredom is thought to take. One empirical study identifies five types, based, dispiritingly, on the study of young people in academic environments. Its first is "indifferent boredom," which comes with some untroubling qualities, such as "relaxation and cheerful fatigue," "a general indifference to, and withdrawal from, the external world." Second is "calibrating boredom," which likewise seems more than bearable, with its subjects experiencing "wandering thoughts," no sense of what they should do, yet quite open to possibilities that might change their immediate situation. A mild enough restlessness is found in "searching boredom," where alternative courses are actively sought. What appears to be a more aggressive version of "searching boredom" is labeled "reactant boredom," where those who experience it not only imagine other circumstances but activate thoughts of escape from their immediate situations. And finally the research identifies the phenomenon of "apathetic boredom," which has "low arousal" and is, it is claimed, "an emotion type more similar to learned helplessness or depression."[3] Two of these types—"indifferent" and "calibrating"—seem to hint at the free qualities of idleness, which is notable, given that boredom is not usually considered to be an agreeable state. It appears, rather, that there is a misdescription here in that the experiences at issue are not actually boring. It might be more precise to conclude that the individuals concerned are not stimulated by what they are expected to do—concentrate in class and learn—and their minds drift. This might amount to a waste of time from an educational point of view, but its easefulness hardly aligns it with boredom.

A more persuasive typology is reported by Lars Svendsen, who offers us four categories of boredom: "... situative boredom, as when one is waiting for someone, is listening to a lecture or taking the train; the boredom of satiety, when one gets too much of the same thing and everything becomes banal; existential boredom, where the soul is without content and the world is in neutral; and creative boredom, which is not so much characterized by its content as its result: that one is forced to do something new."[4] The first three types are to be regarded as unambivalently disagreeable, though for the different reasons noted in the descriptions. For the purposes of a discussion of boredom that is geared toward the issue of idleness, I want to simplify and slightly revise this typology, proceeding without any complacency about the strictness of the boundaries that are created in defining them. Those boundaries are likely to shift according to our phenomenological acuity and descriptive talents.

Since the "boredom of satiety" looks like an application of "situative boredom" rather than a distinctive type, and "creative boredom" is not, it appears, an experience of boredom at all, I will set them aside. So I will speak only of what I call "circumstantial" boredom, tedium in short, and "existential" boredom. None of the types we have seen so far note the painful experience of tedium that perhaps represents the most immediately unappealing feature of boredom. This is contained in what I am calling "circumstantial boredom," a type that occurs when we are deprived of the opportunity to do what would interest us and are forced at the very same time to do something that does not satisfy us at all. In these situations we are clear enough about what is causing us to be bored, and we expect to be released from boredom as soon as specific circumstances change. This category is obviously close to what others describe as situational boredom, but since "tedium" is placed at its center, a different name perhaps avoids confusion. Peter Toohey captures the tedium of boredom with the following properties: "lengthy duration," "predictability," and "confinement."[5] With regard to duration, we might instead believe that it is possible to have the most tedious of experiences that last only a few moments but that come with the tortuous feeling that the confinement involved could go on forever. Indeed, this sense of tedium, if characterized as confinement, can, as James Geiwitz suggests, be distinguished from the boredom of satiety: "satiation is a point at which a subject will voluntarily reject the task whereas boredom occurs if the subject is compelled to remain at the task after the satiation point."[6] The satiation point might be very quickly reached in some cases. In this light, individuals are not really caught up in boredom when placed in a voluntary relation to the options in front of them unless they are denied flight from those options (that denial is a central plank of the unpleasantness of tedium). The capacity for escape through reverie or imagination saves the disengaged students, whom we saw above, from boredom as such.

There is a kind of opaque boredom that can appear in the midst of everyday existence that is in principle distinguishable from tedium. This "existential" variety, also noted by Svendsen and others, is not necessarily long-lasting or biographically defining. At certain times we may have our judgment affected by a mood that leads us to believe that life has nothing of interest to offer us. At the same time, we do not really know what would interest us. We feel no motivation or capacity to find pleasing activities, none of which are, in any case, conceivable from within the perspective we fall into during this type of boredom. Perhaps it is too grand to call what is described here "existential," as it might actually be a quickly passing state of mind, one that temporarily though inexplicably leaves the sufferer with a displeasing sense of seeing nothing to do. However, the very value of life itself can seem doubtful when we are bored in this way. This is a negative and not merely apathetic condition. This type of boredom seems essentially similar to the aesthetically grand or socially elite phenomenon of "ennui," an experience of estrangement from things in which "the world is emptied of its significance."[7] Its meaninglessness is not to be attributed to any cause, and hence it is not, again, explained in terms of contingent situations or circumstances.

The epistemological differences between these two forms of boredom—circumstantial and existential—are obviously profound: respectively, the knowledge and absence of knowledge of what would relieve the boredom. There is also a notable difference at the level of affect. Agitation is typical of circumstantial boredom or tedium: there is a wish to escape from the commitment that circumstances have imposed. Numerous other possibilities may seem desirable from the perspective of constraint. By contrast, a kind of depressing lethargy is characteristic of the existential form. It is not restful, since those who relate to it reflectively will be troubled by this boredom. It seems misleading that our ordinary language should label as boredom two such differing forms of experience. A broad unifying element might be located in their shared feeling of oppression connected with a frustrated wish to act. A popular view among theorists is that boredom has curative properties. This thesis starts from the sanguine view that the human organism is geared toward enhancing its general well-being. According to this approach, boredom has a function: it is educative in that it provides us with insights into what might be meaningful to us. Boredom is therefore a valuable experience.[8] Or we might less warmly see it as "an adaptive emotion" that "exists to help you prosper"—indeed flourish—by alerting "you to situations that can do no psychological good."[9] It is not clear, though, how broadly this affirmative theory can apply to boredom experiences, other than to those of tedium. The latter, as suggested above, has epistemic content, communicating to us what we find intolerable in our situations.

SCHOPENHAUER ON THE IMPOSSIBILITY OF REST

For Schopenhauer, boredom is not symptomatic of misdirected activity. It is therefore not to be perceived as an opportunity for growth in self-knowledge. Boredom is, rather, the immediate experience of the miserable emptiness of existence. Its sheer awfulness drives us to activity, but not, whatever we might usually believe, in order to make meaningful lives for ourselves. Rather, we act simply to escape from boredom. This general idea motivates Schopenhauer's complex account of human action, which, among other things, offers to explain—as a supposed fact of nature—why human beings cannot endure idleness. Idleness in his view necessarily creates boredom. The worry about idleness as a gateway to boredom is not, obviously enough, exclusive to Schopenhauer. His efforts to defend this association, however, are unique in their depth, encompassing a theory of human psychology and an account of how we human beings are placed within the universe.

As we explore the elements of Schopenhauer's theory, we shall begin to see that its force owes much to a preferred notion of human character. He is committed to subsuming all the human activity that he observes under *homo volens*: we are essentially creatures who simply want. As a consequence of this model, we can, he insists, enjoy states of idleness only momentarily, if at all, since wanting is our most powerful and prevailing motivation. The implausibility of this view is effectively conceded by Schopenhauer himself when he discusses certain forms of experience that are precisely a withdrawal from restless wanting. Of significance too, in assessing Schopenhauer's view about the connection between idleness and boredom, is his ahistorical perspective. Schopenhauer does not consider whether there are specific historical conditions that make that connection more likely. No question is raised about a possible relation between the presence of certain social values and the "fact" that we are by nature restless. Again, though, in other contexts—primarily in his discussion of Cynicism—he implicitly realizes that there are ways of life that successfully detach themselves from the overbearing norms of success and, consequently, from the urge to work and to gain standing in the world. His philosophy might be seen, in this respect, to have an answer to the very problem it appears to bind itself to, namely, whether human beings can free themselves from the social— not natural—pressures to be industrious, productive, and visible.

Schopenhauer holds that life's fundamental state is that of suffering. This claim sits alongside his apparently related view that life is essentially empty. Suffering is attributed neither to individual misfortune and choices nor to historical forces. The cause of the manner in which we human beings suffer is our own intrinsic nature. Our psychological dispositions are structured in such a way that suffering is an ineradicable likelihood. We constantly and uncontrollably, he insists, put ourselves in the way of disappointment. The set of unhappy human experiences is not necessarily greater than the happy one, but it is to be understood as normal rather than aberrant. This means, Schopenhauer believes, that we should consider suffering to be our given condition. It is in that sense "positive." We may sometimes negate or avert that "positive" through distractions of various kinds, but these negative states—periods of contentment—are never lasting. They are temporary interruptions that have the effect of obscuring to us the truth of our condition. The truth is that human life is not essentially happy, meaningful, or tranquil. At best it can cloak itself in these qualities. He develops this picture of human life in considerable detail.

According to Schopenhauer, the structure of boredom consists of *willing without an object*. After we have taken possession of the objects we desired, the will does not cease to exert itself. We go on willing, but sometimes without any particular object in mind. This empty willing is a misery. He explains: "[I]ndeed, when at last all wishes are exhausted, the pressure of will itself remains, even without any recognized motive, and makes itself known with terrible pain as a

feeling of the most frightful desolation and emptiness." Schopenhauer also describes this experience as a
"fearful, life-destroying boredom, a lifeless longing
without a definite object, a deadening languor." A difficulty of personal management is somehow to find
engaging challenges with which to occupy ourselves,
as boredom is, he claims, "always ready to fill up every
pause granted by care."[10]

The Cycle of Human Action

Schopenhauer thinks of normal human life as a constant series of cycles. The dynamic behind these cycles
is a kind of striving or drive of the "will." The will,
roughly speaking, is for Schopenhauer the life force he
believes to be inherent in all things. It is this force that
unsettles any attempt we make to come to peace and
rest. These cycles contain what we might see as several
phases. The order in which we make our way through
these phases does not appear to be reversible. It is reasonably clear that he regards the first phase of the cycle
as desire, and this is followed by pursuit, then satisfaction, and a renewal of desire. If, however, a new desire
does not present itself at the end of satisfaction, we fall
into boredom. Schopenhauer puts it this way: "Now
the nature of man consists in the fact that his will
strives, is satisfied, strives anew, and so on and on; in
fact his happiness and well-being consist only in the
transition from desire to satisfaction, and from this to

a fresh desire, such transition going forward rapidly. For the non-appearance of satisfaction is suffering; the empty longing for a new desire is languor, boredom."[11] Idleness is the state in which we have no project that can absorb us. It is experienced as boredom—the absence of something to do—rather than as a pleasing state of rest. What Schopenhauer describes here appears to be a variety of what we have called existential boredom. In these states, nothing of interest presents itself to us, and we feel incapable of finding anything that would be worth doing. We know this frustrating state of affairs would be resolved were we to undertake a fresh project, but we are also aware that we are not receptive to any course of action that might suggest itself or be proposed to us. That lack of receptivity is, perhaps, the mood itself.

Schopenhauer sometimes uses the term "willing" to capture both the general striving process that moves the cycle of human action—indeed, of all the forces in the universe—and the more specific act of desire. To avoid confusion, the term "desire" will be used here when speaking of willing as a phase of the cycle. Desire, for Schopenhauer, is a powerfully felt need for some object in particular. Each desire, though, is itself a misery, since it is about something we want yet do not have. He has in mind the painful edge of the experience of privation. He writes that "every desire springs from a need, a want, a suffering."[12] Schopenhauer assumes that the telic nature of desires—that they seek some end—allows us to have extended periods of distraction. During the efforts that are required to gain the objects of desire, boredom is pushed away.

It may, though, seem puzzling that Schopenhauer should interpret desire as the solution we find for our boredom. He maintains that we ultimately escape the torments of boredom—objectless willing—by moving to desire, itself another kind of suffering. As he puts it, desire is "nothing more than a change" of the "form" in which suffering comes to us.[13] In idle boredom the restless will has no object with which to occupy itself, whereas in desire an object is selected. The absence of that object represents an existing lack in the subject. Both states are marked by a painful feeling of absence, though of quite different kinds: respectively, the absence of an object to desire and the absence in one's life of the object desired. Schopenhauer thinks, though, of desire and boredom as the twin forces of motivation that keep human beings "in motion":[14] there is the striving for objects that is characteristic of all life, and there is the fear of boredom, which prevents rest.

The idea of a transition from boredom to desire appears, nevertheless, to be misguided. Desire, itself a form of suffering, does not look, on the face of it, to be a solution to boredom. Is boredom the most awful of all experiences? Worse than the biting sense of lack that Schopenhauer attributes to desire? Now one of Schopenhauer's most fundamental claims is that we human beings are ignorant of the motivations and driving principles that make us work. We wrongly take ourselves to be latent idlers who are "inwardly indolent [*träge*]" and long "for rest" from desire. In order for us to live in something like contented idleness, in Schopenhauer's view, "it would also be necessary for a fundamental change to occur in man himself, and hence for him to be no longer what he is, but rather to become what he is not."[15] It is simply a supposed fact of nature that idleness is precluded to us. His reply to the question above (about desire as a solution to boredom) will therefore be that we are creatures who are continually impelled toward what makes us miserable even as we consciously, though naively, pursue it in the name of happiness. As Schopenhauer puts it: "Every immoderate joy (*exultatio, insolens laetitia*) always rests on the delusion that we have found something in life that is not to be met with at all, namely permanent satisfaction of the tormenting desires or cares that constantly breed new ones"[16] A new desire is, allegedly, a renewal of that very delusion. It does not intentionally target what it expects will turn out to be merely temporary contentment.

Desire, Schopenhauer claims, is followed by the pleasantly absorbing experience of *pursuit* of the object desired. At this point in the cycle there is hope that the object can be won. How realistic that might be is irrelevant. Once the pursuit is brought to a successful conclusion, there is the agreeable feeling of *satisfaction*. Schopenhauer designates this pleasure, and the associated experience of pursuit, as "negative" states in that they are the negation of the basic, "positive" (empty and suffering) state of existence. Pleasure is preceded by painful desiring, and pain reenters when the phases of pursuit and satisfactory attainment reach their conclusion. Once the object is gained, its value evaporates: "[A]ttainment quickly begets satiety. The goal was only apparent; possession takes away its charm."[17] The value that we placed in the object was mistaken, as pleasure was located more or less solely in our efforts to capture that object. The object, whatever it might be, has no intrinsic value. This is consistent with Schopenhauer's more general thesis that there are no intrinsic goods. As Bernard Reginster points out, if, for Schopenhauer, "anything in our existence had value 'in itself,' its possession would be a positive good, rather than merely the absence of the pain caused by the need for it."[18] And this would contradict Schopenhauer's view that there is no positive good in the world, a view that is sustained by his claim that suffering alone is positive. All those things we take to be good are merely extrinsically good. They are entirely relative to our desire for them. And those efforts arise from our need to avoid boring idleness. Schopenhauer's primary examples of these extrinsic goods are sensual pleasure and the pursuit of esteem.

Schopenhauer knows that we may move immediately from satisfaction to a new desire. The cycle of human action can renew itself without pause. Individuals who seamlessly move from task to task certainly never idle and may have little experience of boredom. Satisfaction with an object, it could be suggested, might in fact stimulate further desire for that object, though this may be precluded by Schopenhauer's idea that there are no intrinsic goods. Or a desire for a wholly new object could, with good fortune, quickly take root. In either way, the cycle is smoothly renewed, and the negative state of happiness is preserved: "[H]appiness and well-being," Schopenhauer writes, "consist only in the transition from desire to satisfaction, and from this to a fresh desire, such transition going forward rapidly."[19] However, this transition is not certain. Nothing in the satisfied experience, Schopenhauer believes, necessarily anticipates further pleasure. If desire cannot immediately identify a new object to pursue, then we are idle and boredom immediately begins. Boredom pushes human beings into evasive action, with merit found in that action only if it is sufficiently distracting. A striking example of distraction not motivated by any ideal is the creation of human society itself: "Boredom . . . causes beings who love one another as little as men do, to seek one another so much, and thus becomes the source of sociability."[20] But there are less elevated cases too. The "*ozio lungo d'uomini ignoranti*"—unlike the leisure of those who know how to use their time—is driven by purely "trivial motives." The "man of limited intelligence" finds the simplest of distractions, such as "rattling and drumming with anything he can get hold of."[21]

Is Boredom Inevitable?

Schopenhauer, then, does not accept the possibility of idle pleasure, that is, of pleasurable experience that is not caught up in the cycle of human endeavor. After the efforts we undertake to gain "hard-won leisure [*Muße*]," we find only boredom and "dullness." Idleness, which is desirable because it seems to rescue us from external demands and to place us in "possession" of ourselves, ultimately imposes a "burden" because it is in constant conflict with the restlessness of our natures.[22] This restlessness, though, does not seem to hold true for a significant range of human experiences. Considerations of lasting pleasures are strangely absent from Schopenhauer's study of behavior. And Schopenhauer, as Ivan Soll notes, tends to confuse satisfaction with satiety.[23] A satisfying experience need not entail the exhaustion of that experience. Among the lasting pleasures are loving relationships and sheer delight in the presence of what one finds beautiful. Any one of these experiences might be considered idle, though. They have no *telos*: they are enjoyable in themselves, are unproductive, require no effort, and are not easily reducible to the status of "distractions." Either Schopenhauer neglects these experiences, or he takes them to be composed of a series of distinctive pleasures: they are then a sequence like any other, except in this case one object, rather than a diversity, is central to them. If this is the way Schopenhauer thinks of long-lasting pleasures, it is self-evidently false to experience. He does, in fact, have much to say about beauty when he urges a transformation in our relation to things: aesthetic experience is contemplative and contrasts with the usual efforts to devour the world. However, when he speaks of boredom, that domain is

absent from his analysis. We are left with the assertion
that experiences have a determinate and psychologi-
cally challenging endpoint.

Of particular relevance to this study is Schopenhauer's effort to gain ground for the necessity of the
idleness-boredom connection by overlooking significant distinctions within the phenomenon of boredom
itself. His assumption that idleness inflicts a burden
on us seems to be sustained by his belief that idleness
is, in effect, tedium. This is highlighted in an example
he provides in the name of unmasking the delusory
appeal of idleness: "The strict penitentiary system of
Philadelphia makes mere boredom an instrument of
punishment through loneliness and idleness [*Un-
thätigkeit*]. It is so terrible an instrument, that it has
brought convicts to suicide."[24] This illustration is obviously more complicated than it seems. First, it does
not appear to resonate with boredom as empty willing. The sufferer is not epistemically ignorant and
does not seek distraction. The prisoner has a clear object in mind too: freedom from jail or the company of
others. The phenomenon, then, is not, in other words,
empty willing but willing whose objective realization
has been denied by circumstances. Second, it con-
strues idleness as the tedium of "circumstantial" boredom. As a consequence, the horrors of enforced idleness are no different, in Schopenhauer's view, from
those situations in which there is nothing purposeful
to do. However, in enforced situations the agent of
our misery is someone else (e.g., the jailer).

Schopenhauer holds, in effect, that the absence of any motivating desires—the experience of empty willing—can throw us into situations in which we feel a kind of imposition that is at least analogous if not identical with tedium. This experience is caused by the pressure of the will. The imposition we might identify in boring idleness, once the cycle of action has been completed, is not then more truly to be attributed to circumstances that the world has inflicted on us—for example, solitary confinement, a repetitive task, a boring conversation. It is produced by our own reaction to the absence of desirable activity. In this respect we become our own tormentors. This torment is attributable to a blind human urge for activity.

The motivations for this activity are, as we have seen, entirely internal: the will. But Schopenhauer lets slip a more credible account of what might lie at the back of what drives us. It is more credible in that it can, contrary to his naturalistic line, accommodate the reality that idleness is not inevitably a precursor to boredom. When we are idle, we are absent from what Schopenhauer claims is the most important enterprise of all, that of increasing our social visibility and winning the regard of other people: "Folly goes to such lengths, and the opinion of others is a principal aim of the efforts of everyone, although the complete futility of this is expressed by the fact that in almost all languages vanity, *vanitas*, originally signifies emptiness and nothingness."[25] If esteem is of such persistent significance to us, we might wonder how the experience of empty willing is possible. Of immediate interest here, though, is that Schopenhauer has aligned much of our striving with the game of social achievement. One possible inference from this is that a collapse in our commitment to that game might equally weaken our tendency to restlessness, precisely because it removes one of the motivations that lie behind the restlessness of boredom.

Schopenhauer does not offer that particular conclusion, believing, officially at least, that this restlessness is not in fact caused by any phenomenon of the world. It is caused by the will. If we recall the various claims made by Hegel, in particular, on usefulness and practical education, we might have another way of interpreting what Schopenhauer sees as the empty will. To the properly socialized individual there is, Hegel maintains, the self-perpetuating need to be occupied. If he is right, we can go further and suggest that boredom looms when this need is not met. After all, it is only the un-socialized savage, it was claimed, who idles without unhappiness. Schopenhauer, though, directs his investigation toward truths that, in his view, have nothing to do with historical social conditions. We must see past the appearance of "endless changes and their chaos and confusion" and analyze instead "the same, identical, unchangeable essence, acting in the same way today as it did yesterday and always."[26]

Schopenhauer nevertheless acknowledges, in spite of this essentialist thinking, that escape from the pain of empty willing is possible and can be achieved if we extricate ourselves from the pressures of social expectation. He commends the teachings of the Cynics. He admires their "defiance" of the "strange tricks" that happiness plays on us and their insight into the torments inflicted by desire.[27] The Cynics realized that happiness was not to be gained by the pursuit of desire, but by the rejection of all desires. This may appear to be consistent with Schopenhauer's general view of the dismal cycle of life, but it is in another respect a curious and contradictory concession in that it allows that it might just be possible for us to find a sort of happiness by renouncing the usual avenues of pleasure. One might expect the Cynics' way of life to be a bleak one, marked by the ceaseless resistance to pleasure. But, in fact, as Schopenhauer tells us, their lives were quite otherwise. Indeed, what he describes looks like a liberating idleness: "They spent their time in resting, walking about, talking with everyone, and in scoffing, laughing, and joking. Their characteristics were heedlessness and great cheerfulness."[28] But how could this be? Because what they secured through renunciation was "independence." It would hardly capture the cheerfulness of the Cynic were we to think of that independence as the outcome of fearsome asceticism. The happiness the Cynic achieves involves fundamentally a withdrawal from the pursuit of social prestige (a recommendation Schopenhauer also finds in Rousseau's thoughts on the origins of inequality). As Schopenhauer reports, they "did not work" and "had no aims of their own, no purposes and intentions to pursue, and so were lifted above human activities, and at the same time always enjoyed complete leisure."[29] Idleness is a realistic possibility after all. No doubt, it requires a certain type of personality to be willing to withdraw from the processes that drive us in organized societies. But what Schopenhauer concedes is that adherence to those processes is not inevitable. We can, in fact, bring those processes into question and perhaps extricate ourselves from the demands they place upon us. And we can do so without falling necessarily into the dreaded state of boredom.

Schopenhauer himself knows that the misery he associates with frustrated desire has something to do with our socialization, and that it is possible to liberate ourselves from that frustration, as the Cynics' example shows. This insight could have prompted further thought about the kinds of pressures that are imposed on us through the forms of social interaction we take to be normal. Instead, as we have seen, he tells us that we experience boredom when we cannot find some desire, a desire that may be of a sort that turns out to be the means for gaining a standing in "the opinion of others." The answer to this misery is, though, known to the Cynics: we escape that misery by disregarding the value of the demand that generates those desires.

Schopenhauer's acknowledgment of the emptiness of caring about "the opinion of others" and his appreciation of the significance of the Cynics have not been discussed here in order to convict him of inconsistency. Rather, these claims are useful to us in that they have given us a means by which to interrogate the notion that we can never truly be happy while idle. This insight cannot serve to change the psychology of those who think that idleness is boring. It does, though, at least allow us to gain a perspective that can weaken the apparent natural necessity that is thought to sustain the boredom-idleness connection. The restless feeling that we must keep ourselves occupied may, for some at least, be the call of social prestige. Or perhaps it is to be attributed, more basically still, to the practical natures that education and discipline inculcate in us.

THE IMAGE OF THE IDLE WOMAN

Friedrich Nietzsche and Søren Kierkegaard draw, in different ways, a significant distinction between men and women in terms of their capacities for boredom and idleness. Intrinsic attributes, they implicitly maintain, underpin a supposed peculiar capacity of women, in contrast with men, to be unaffected by boredom. This positions women to enjoy idleness in some manner that men cannot. Nietzsche shares with Schopenhauer the thesis that human beings are restless. Unlike Schopenhauer, however, he explicitly finds some connection between one aspect of our social formation and our inability to idle. The aspect in question is work:

Need compels us to perform work with the proceeds of which the need is assuaged; need continually recurs and we are thus accustomed to working. In the intervals, however, during which our needs have been assuaged and are as it were sleeping, we are overtaken by boredom. What is this? It is our habituation to work as such, which now asserts itself as a new, additional need; and the more strongly habituated we are to working, perhaps even the more we have suffered need, the stronger this new need will be. To elude boredom man either works harder than is required to satisfy his other needs or he invents play, that is to say work designed to assuage no other need than the need for work as such.[30]

If one of the conditions of boredom is work habituation, we might expect that condition itself to be the subject of analysis. This is not, however, the direction Nietzsche takes. He focuses on the conditions in which human beings could enjoy idleness without the intrusions of boredom. In one specific context at least he identifies idleness as an admirable quality, but it is one that belongs to individuals who have, in some way, overcome their socialization. Those who can idle, in this sense, are supposedly above those industrious types who remain enslaved to their work (and are therefore, we might infer, vulnerable to boredom). Speaking "in favour of the idle [*Müßigen*]," Nietzsche declares that "there is something noble about leisure and idleness [*Muße und Müßiggehen*]." It is "the idle man" specifically who "is always a better man than the active."[31]

With his usual enmity, Nietzsche holds that women who idle do not, however, have the same significance. Rather, their idleness is explained in terms of a deficiency. Women, he thinks, stand at a pre-social level: "Many people, especially women, never feel boredom because they have never learned to work properly."[32] It appears, then, that there are in fact two kinds of idleness: the higher one, experienced by people who have exercised an advanced capacity in making themselves independent of the demands of the world, and the lower one, which falls to the poorly trained. (Nietzsche does not comment on whether there are men who idle peacefully through lack of education.) The assumption that sustains this latter distinction is a familiar one in modern thought, one we have seen in other philosophers discussed in this book. It is the difference between those who are perceived to determine themselves and those who are not. The experience of the latter group is not to be applauded or envied if it is merely the product of circumstances over which it has no control, even when its experience resembles that of the group that is placed above it.

Nietzsche's conception of the idle women is likely to refer to women of the wealthier social classes of his times, though he does not quite explain which sort of person he has in mind. We know that many women living within that broad class did not work outside the home, nor, for respectability's sake, could they be seen to take on domestic chores. To the unfriendly eye— such as Nietzsche's—their world might seem to be filled with idleness. That perception, though, misses the reality of what we now recognize as dependency and implicit servility. And it does not consider either the arduousness of keeping up appearances, a demand that belies the supposed idleness of the bourgeois woman.

Kierkegaard—or at least the aesthetic persona of his *Either/Or*—is captivated by the appearance of genteel feminine idleness. He proposes that women are admirably suited to idleness without boredom. Women, in this regard, stand in contrast with those human beings who, like restless "brutes," are constantly "on the move." These brutes—men of business especially—aggressively engage the world. They have no interest in experiencing life passively. They strive ceaselessly to turn every opportunity to their advantage. Lacking a capacity for idleness, they will quickly fall into boredom when not wrestling with the world. Kierkegaard's aesthete, then, seems to believe that boredom and idleness mutually exclude each other. Individuals who cannot idle are subject to boredom. And those with a capacity for idleness, it turns out, do not suffer from boredom. In support of that claim Kierkegaard cites the example of the "Olympian Gods," who "were not bored, they lived happily in happy idleness." He also presents, in sharp contrast with the uncouth businessman, the case of the "beautiful woman, who neither sews nor spins nor bakes nor reads nor plays the piano" but who "is happy in her idleness, for she is not bored."[33]

The complexity of Kierkegaard's narrative stance leaves open the possibility that the aesthete—qua aesthete—is ironically exposed as blind to the reality of female "idleness," naively praising what is merely an appearance. Equally—and not necessarily in opposition—the view reflects a kind of aesthetic idealization of what he takes to be pure femininity and its barely attainable perfection. Entailed in this perspective is the ultimately demeaning opinion that the glory of womanhood is found when women are—as the line above suggests—unencumbered by education or skills. Unlike certain kinds of men "whose whole life is business,"[34] and who consequently are at risk of boredom, the "beautiful woman" does nothing and is blissfully happy. Kierkegaard's text offers us the image of a woman utterly unmoved by the world and certainly not formed by it. She transcends the mundane reality of work and business. This is, obviously enough, a fanciful account of social arrangements that plays—ironically or otherwise—with the surfaces.

Boredom and the Idle Woman

Beauvoir does not discuss the texts we have just examined. Nonetheless, her account of what she refers to as "*la femme oisive*"—the idle woman—helps to expose the basis of the deceptive image of the idling and simple beauty. Beauvoir's main contention is that supposed feminine idleness is generated by the unequal ways in which women are expected to occupy the institution of marriage. She is interested in particular in those arrangements where the husband's economic advantages mean that the wife loses any compelling reason to take up outside employment. Marriage seems to free women from work and to allow them the freedom to idle as they please. In this context idleness—*oisiveté*—acquires, though, purely negative meanings. It does not refer to a state of satisfying detachment from the empty purposes of the world. Rather, because of the circumstances in which it arises, idleness has the effect of an imposition. It deprives women of the opportunity to acquire the capabilities through which they might realize themselves in ways Beauvoir considers authentic.

Beauvoir's claims are especially pertinent to middle-class European life during the time of her own writing. (*The Second Sex* was published in 1949.) She stands at a period of transition in which the wife's abstention from a career is not essential to the dignity of the family. Yet neither does the analysis cover a time in which equality has become a matter of great public concern. A number of reasons, connected to the status of the husband, lie behind the decision by women to spend most of their mature lives in the family home. The supposed goods that are attached to work are not, Beauvoir observes, available to all. Women, she claims,

take up employment primarily for its monetary benefits. Men, though, work not only for financial reasons
but also to establish visible social identities. This dis-
parity is not a matter of nature, but of expectation
based on the quite differing levels of professional recognition men and women might hope to receive. The
possibility of achieving a respected identity—indeed
dignity—through non-domestic activities is open essentially to men alone. The inverse course is effectively
determined for women. A further element that weighs
against a wife's decision to seek out a career is the competitive prestige gained by those husbands who are
seen to be able to afford to keep their wives away from
the world of work.

Alongside these implicit factors, in which the career interests of women are secondary to those of men,
is the beguiling and delusive prospect of blissful idleness that marriage might bring. In fact, Beauvoir sees
that prospect as exerting the greatest damage on the
independence of women: "It has not been sufficiently
realized that the temptation is also an obstacle, and
even one of the most dangerous. Here a hoax is involved, since in fact there will be only one winner out
of thousands in the lottery of marriage. The present
epoch invites, even compels women to work; but it
flashes before their eyes paradises of idleness and delight: it exalts the winners far above those who remain
tied down to earth."[35]

Women wonder whether to choose paid employment, an advance in independence though it offers

them little recognition, or a marriage of luxurious leisure. Idleness, however it might turn out in reality, seems to be an attractive way of life. It is regarded as a prize of some kind. Gaining the latter is, though, no easy task. It is not really a matter of pure luck either. To enter the "lottery," as Beauvoir puts it, a woman must take on those qualities that "please men."[36] Those qualities will include a willingness to cede her independence in favor of the greater career interests and status of the husband. Part of what femininity means is tied not only to a particular kind of physical appearance and manners but also to seeming to be the kind of person who—unlike her busy male partner—can be content with doing nothing. The consequences for the woman as a person who might, under other circumstances, have developed in complexity and capacities through her own free self-determining choices are profound. Beauvoir quotes Jules Laforgue: "Since she has been left in slavery, idleness [*la paresse*], without occupation or weapon other than her sex, she has over-developed this aspect and has become the Feminine. . . . We have permitted this hypertrophy; she is here in the world for our benefit. . . . Well! that is all wrong. . . . Up to now we have played with Woman as if she were a doll."[37]

It is this doll-like existence that, perhaps, Kierkegaard's aesthete takes to be a virtuous one. The reality that lies behind it, according to Beauvoir, is a life of "horrible idleness," which becomes more sharply painful as the woman ages and no longer has around her the children who once absorbed her time.[38] Because she is without developed skills and experience of sustained work—a consequence of her formation as a woman eligible for marriage—she will not be equipped to apply herself to tasks that meaningfully absorb her. Application is a capacity that is gained, Beauvoir like others holds, only through training and persistence. She illustrates this point with the example of the artistic endeavors of once "idle" women: "Even if she begins fairly early, she seldom envisages art as serious work; accustomed to idleness, having never felt in her mode of life the austere necessity of discipline, she will not be capable of sustained and persistent effort, she will never succeed in gaining a solid technique."[39]

Art is, in this case, a hobby whose purpose is little more than to pass the time. The notion of someone who "dabbles" is implied here. The woman's creative efforts, Beauvoir says, do not "extend her grasp on the world, but only . . . relieve her boredom."[40] Her art is inauthentic in aesthetic terms, since it does not express the woman's sense of herself or of the world. (Though the sociologically minded observer might nevertheless be able to recognize what those art works say about the situation of the woman.) Expression of that order requires just that dedicated character and technical ability whose possibility "the idle woman" has necessarily surrendered.

Beauvoir's account of the idle woman might be thought to serve as a warning against the appeal of idleness. Certainly the experience of this problematic idler challenges the skepticism with which I have approached a number of philosophical efforts to denigrate idleness. The phenomenon is so well described that it invites the conclusion that idleness is self-defeating in profound ways: it nullifies the very capacities that keep us from boredom and therefore ensures that idleness becomes unpleasant. Furthermore, Beauvoir effectively supports those philosophers who see opposition between idleness and the genuine freedom they associate with disciplined self-determination. After all, women in the context Beauvoir describes are—it is claimed—indifferent to what they will make of themselves (Kant) other than what makes them appealing to prospective husbands. Nor do they have a background of "practical education" (Hegel), it also appears. The product of these factors is, eventually, bored idleness once women are left with time they must fill on their own initiative. Their experience brings Schopenhauer's account of boredom to mind: empty time can be filled only through the pursuit of activities whose significance lies purely in their negation of emptiness.

The situation of the idle woman, however, does not allow us to draw decisive conclusions about the general nature of idleness. At the center of the woman's experience, as we have seen it described, is a comparatively limited scope for freedom and certainly for self-determination. The conventional available choice gears the woman toward a single outcome. The decision not to develop an enriching set of career skills means in this context adopting instead the role of a kind of elite idler, of someone who does not need to work. This is not, though, equivalent ultimately to an ability to idle pleasurably since it is idleness required by the norms of an institution. The woman *must* idle. Idleness is not then a freedom here but a mode of conformity. It comes with the attendant loss of the woman's ability to regard herself as an individual with independent interests. Those interests may come into view at a particular phase of family life. A vulnerability to helpless boredom at that phase is the result of an institutionalized idle neglect of personal development. What we might learn from this situation is that idleness becomes a liberating possibility only where individuals secede from or perhaps never belong to institutions. These options have been unsuccessfully dismissed by philosophers—as we have seen—as either impossible or primitive. Clearly a Diogenean escape is an unrealistic possibility for the idle woman Beauvoir describes. But again, what is brought primarily into view by that difficulty should be the overwhelming force of the institution rather than the incompatibility of idleness with freedom.

CHAPTER 4

PLAY AS IDLENESS

One of the lessons we are supposed to take from the philosophical complaints about idleness is that properly formed human beings need to be committed to a course of action or perhaps a rational plan of life. Experience, for a number of reasons, cannot follow the random paths of idleness. Without the right kind of self-occupation we may fail in our duties to ourselves, denigrate our potential for autonomy, defy our communal being, or simply suffer from boredom. The very idea of idleness is also dismissed on grounds that are quite separate from grandiose theories of self-constitution and the like. It faces, above all, the objection that an idle existence is impractical for beings like us. To idle means obviously that we do not work. Even if we reject those philosophical claims about the glories of labor, we are still confronted with a practical reality: things need to get done. There may be discomfort and inconvenience involved in addressing basic needs, but we are more than accustomed to that reality. We may idle as long as we do not forget how to work.

There is, however, one strand of thought that, in effect, tries to think beyond the tension between work and idleness. Rather, these forms of life can be brought into unity, not merely into balance. That unity is thought to ground a new but truly human freedom, one that embodies spontaneity and the absence of all preconceived purpose. The name of this free behavior is "play." Play holds a marginal place in the theoretical literature on alternatives to the ideal of *homo laborans*. In the context of the perceived limitations of the idleness model, play does, though, deserve close attention. Play, like idleness, appears to be free from the pressures that mark out life today. And it has relatively little social value when compared with the earnestness with which we are supposed to develop our talents and realize our uses. As Russell notes, "there was formerly a capacity for light-heartedness and play which has been to some extent inhibited by the cult of efficiency."[1] Even so, play, unlike idleness, has not become disreputable. It is not—prima facie—to be dismissed as a mere utopian phenomenon. Many will recognize the possibility of meaningful pleasure in, for example, music, sport, or dance, at least when these activities are playful. The question to be pursued here is whether play can, as a number of philosophers have suggested, give us a plausible picture of human action that is free from the demands for seriousness, usefulness, and self-preoccupation.

A core characteristic of idleness is its freedom from the norms that make effective modern social beings of us. Idleness is never guided by any particular notion of an outcome or of a "self" that is to be realized. Idle actions are spontaneous expressions of what individuals prefer to do as they act within the contexts they have chosen. Most significantly, idleness contrasts with those potentially self-defeating conceptions of life that connect freedom to self-actualization within rule-governed institutions. These conceptions may claim to have discovered the solution to the problem of the tension between what human beings desire and what they must do. Hegel, as we have seen, is an arch proponent of this idea. But what sort of freedom does Hegel's theory really defend when one of its conditions is that we must be made receptive through socialization to those norms that amount to acceptable forms of expressive activity? These norms seem to involve us in necessity: there are certain ways of being or of choosing that we must act upon if we are to be considered free. We may often experience the force of those norms when our inclinations drift toward other desires. But in a good society, such tensions are supposed to be minimal, since what individuals by and large want to do will be what society wants and needs too. In this situation the necessity that is experienced is positive. This good necessity is sometimes thought of as a "higher" type. It elevates us above the base necessity that urges us to follow mere desire or threatening and alien laws. Nevertheless, the harmony that this model supposedly achieves, as just noted, rests on prior socialization. Expressions of freedom are thereby channeled one way rather than another. If we are concerned that this compromises freedom in some respect, then it may be because we believe that there could be an intelligible form of freedom that is free of necessity. It is here that, again, idleness seems to meet that description.

It is not surprising that proponents of play, which is likewise conceived as freedom from necessity, have in mind a form of experience that resembles idleness. Play, like idleness, is offered as an alternative to the inhibiting demands of the world of work. In conception, however, the theory of play—in its anti-work context—is sustained by an ambiguity. In some respects play seems to entail the elimination of necessity (hence its idleness-like quality). But in ascribing to it some specific form, play takes on the quality of higher necessity, that is, higher than the alienating necessities of our current social arrangements or of desire. This ambiguity is evident in the two philosophical theories of play that will be examined in this chapter, those of Schiller and Marcuse. Both Schiller and Marcuse reject the norm of work for work's sake or as an instrument for any good that lies beyond what it immediately produces. Their conceptions of play do not try to defend work, at least not any familiar sense of that activity. These commitments point toward some sense of the idea of freedom as idleness. As we shall see, Schiller appears to acknowledge and value that idea while at the same time ultimately adopting a conclusive position on freedom as higher necessity, a position that cannot accommodate the notion of idleness. Marcuse, for his part, attempts to embed something along the lines of idle playfulness within a radically transformed conception of work. That conception, however, takes on a paradoxical structure that ends up voiding the very meaning of idleness.

In spite of the difficulties that will be uncovered, Schiller and Marcuse are, nevertheless, significant contributors to the discussion of playful idleness. They each recognize that the freedom from necessity that is entailed in idleness becomes possible only through a profound transformation of what it means to be truly human. Both philosophers employ what might be understood as the most advanced theories of their respective times in order to underwrite their proposals for a possible anthropological revolution. Schiller works with the practical idealism of early German idealism, while Marcuse turns to psychoanalytic psychology. Each urges us to see the brutishness of the materialism and dark purpose of his society. But the solutions to those deficiencies can be effective only if human beings themselves take on a wholly new character. That character is marked by a capacity for what, as we shall see, approaches and sometimes explicitly takes the form of idleness.

SCHILLER: PLAY AS IDLENESS

In the *Aesthetic Education of Man* (1795), Schiller sets out for his contemporaries a plan that might prompt a dramatic advance in the quality of freedom that society can enable. Although social institutional arrangements may as they stand be orderly, they cannot, he maintains, be regarded as truly free. We live within a state that like clockwork determines social participation "with meticulous exactitude by means of a formulary which inhibits all freedom of thought."[2] Schiller's prescient image of society is, then, of a kind of whole in which all independence is unknowingly surrendered to the aims of the "system." When freedom is compromised in this way, so too is the moral life. For Schiller, as for Kant, morality is the supreme exercise of freedom. Significantly, though, Schiller departs from Kantian moral theory in most important respects. The Kantian moral agent is for him, in fact, another misrepresentation of freedom. Schiller implies that Kant's notion of moral duty is suited to the psychology of a "barbarian," a form of humanity in which—Schiller notably thinks—"principle destroys feeling."[3] Schiller is attempting to situate morality within what he considers to be a non-Kantian conception of human beings. It is his view that a theory of morality based exclusively on duty and reason is hostile to the totality of human action.[4] A further and perhaps more original worry about the Kantian theory is that it can be effective only when its agents engage in a radical type of self-deception. We might as Kantians, Schiller contends, believe that our motivations come from a rational source, and that we are not influenced by the senses. But human beings are sensuous, and the senses must exert their demands on us regardless of whether we take ourselves to be free of them. If we are deceived, though, we become the unwitting "slave" of the senses.[5] Against Kant, then, Schiller insists that a more holistic conception of what we are must be represented in any credible conception of the moral life and in the political arrangements that are built on that conception.[6]

Schiller claims that if human beings are to become genuinely free and thereby moral, they will first have to pass through an intermediary phase. There is no single leap from the deformities inflicted by the mechanical state to the condition of moral independence. He proposes that the human capacity for "play" might, with the appropriate development, serve as a transitional step between human beings as they now are—creatures whose physical wants incline them toward an essentially material society—to what they can ideally be, namely, moral beings. This, Schiller claims, will enable human beings to elevate themselves from "physical necessity [*Notwendigkeit*] into moral necessity."[7] As readers of *Aesthetic Education* usually notice, however, Schiller commits so much of what he values in freedom to his conception of play that play ceases to look like a transitional phase and becomes, instead, the highest point of human development. That status is expressed in the famous line, "man only plays when he is in the fullest sense of the word a human being."[8] In Schiller's text we see a number of concepts that, in his usages, stand under the general notion of hostile necessity, that is, of necessity that we experience unpleasantly: *Nötigung, Notwendigkeit, Zwang,* or necessity and compulsion. The presence of necessity or compulsion in our experience is, for Schiller (again in opposition to Kant), evidence that we are not truly free.

Schiller generally maintains that play is a freedom marked by a higher and better form of necessity, one that combines and transcends existing forms of necessity. In this respect play does not appear to be compatible with the freedom that is characteristic of idleness: its freedom from all compulsion. Schiller claims that in the very act of bringing together forms of necessity, forms that are specific to experiences of the moral law and of the material world, play negates the unwelcome quality of those experiences. When operating in separation, however, each of those necessities is antagonistic to some feature of the human being as a whole. Formal necessity alienates us from our sensuous being, since its concern is law or principle. That is Kant's mistake. (There is something awkward about the conviction with which Schiller criticizes the difficulties of "formality," since this property ought to be rare in the unfree material society he claims to find around him.) Material necessity, in contrast, stands in the way of moral character, since it excludes from its account of human agency any persistent commitments that shape, rather than simply receive, sensory experiences. In play, though, a productive reconciliation between these necessities is developed.[9]

The Structure of Play

Schiller claims that play reconciles what he takes to be the two fundamental drives of human beings: the sense or material drive and the formal drive. By drive, Schiller means an active orientation toward the outer world. This orientation is determinate. Each drive has a specific interest in the world. The interest of the sense drive lies in sensuous engagement with the outer world. The formal drive involves its agents in bringing order to that world. This contrast between the sense/material and formal drives is sharply drawn. It follows from that contrast that a physical life—in some way determined as it is exclusively through the sense drive—is without form. The "physical man," according to Schiller, can merely feel and desire. His experience is "nothing but world" understood as the "formless content of time."[10] We might imagine, though, that experience in the clockwork state is already formal, destructively formal even, in that it is determined by the social mechanism, as Schiller has said. But Schiller is certainly not suggesting that human behavior should just comply with rules in order to help us overcome the lawlessness of physical motivations. In that context formality would be an imposition—would not be "living form"[11]—and thereby stand in contrast with the moral freedom of the formal drive.

The absence of "form" involves a range of implications. Physical beings as "nothing but world" are, according to Schiller, "merely subservient to the laws of nature."[12] The "physical man" is for that reason passive at the level of his engagement with the actual world. The lines of Schiller's thinking are, on this point, indistinguishable from those of his Jena friend and neighbor, Johann Gottlieb Fichte: a material being is not an agent and is therefore without genuine freedom. However, the fact that the sensuousness of the physical man comes about through a drive that orients him dynamically toward sensuous experience must mean that he is not an object of nature in the paradigm sense. The drive, after all, is active. The physical man therefore deals with the outer world in a particular way. As a creature of immediacy, he responds to the sensory opportunities of the world: his experience consists of feeling.

Schiller thinks that a purely passive creature can experience only ceaseless change. Pure passivity entails, for him, the absence of an agent who might control experience. Beings of this kind do not realize themselves as totalities, living instead in the flow of time. Schiller holds that "everyone is outside himself as long as he does nothing but feel."[13] What he is describing here are the conditions of a chaotic life. But it is clear that he wants us to see that as equivalent to an immoral life. The formal drive, by contrast, seeks to structure experience. It "insists on unity and persistence."[14] We can infer from this that the formal drive relates to what we now think of as "agency." The agent, in this regard, is not "outside himself" but is intentionally engaged with decisions and actions. On the basis of this quite simple model, we can see that Schiller's position is more likely to align idleness with the deficiencies identified with passivity: idleness is certainly not formally structured, and it follows rather than imposes experience on itself.

Accompanying the two drives are two senses of the will. One is capriciousness (*Willkür*), and the other is rational will (*Wille*). The sense drive is connected with caprice. The sensuous individual in some way allows choices to be made through the senses. Caprice takes no direction, its preferences are arbitrary. In this way caprice is passive. It has no view about the desires it wants to have. Its passivity is not, though, analogous to the neutral and causally receptive faculty of the senses. After all, caprice is a form of action, but it proceeds without discrimination, takes in the world as it finds it. Hence Schiller's characterization of "natural man," that is, the man without formation or *Bildung*, as guilty of "making a lawless misuse of his licence [*Willkür*]."[15] Such a man, in other words, surrenders himself to his caprices. This lament is directed against hedonism: the pursuit of unlimited pleasures. It is also, again, an implicit critique of idleness in that it excludes the indifference to what we ought to make of ourselves—how we should improve ourselves according to some ideal of humanity—that marks out idleness against more conventional notions of self-constituting personhood. This perspective is underpinned by the role Schiller ascribes to the rational will. It is free and gives us the power to choose "between duty and inclination."[16] In this way it draws from under us "the ladder of nature," whereas caprice keeps us bound to nature.[17]

The play drive contains the material and formal drives. It allows for a sensuous exercise of freedom that differs from merely capricious material experience. Thanks to its formal dimension, play prepares human beings for the consummate point of existence, namely, moral existence. Moral existence is understood by Schiller to involve formal, law-governed agency. His notion of formality is put to considerable work here in that it is supposed to encompass a broad type of human behavior that freely operates within prescribed rules. For Schiller this includes morality, of course, but also athletic competition and aesthetic creativity. The status of this supposed third drive is, though, unclear. Eva Schaper helpfully suggests that the play drive is not in fact a "real" drive at all, in the sense that the two fundamental drives are, but is "emergent," becoming effective—in ways unexplained—when the necessities imposed by the two fundamental drives cease to "dominate" and by some means harmonize with one another.[18] Schiller maintains that this "emergent" drive combines the fullest exercise of the formal and sense drives. The latter opens us to the "infinitude of phenomena" while the former enables us to bring unity to that infinitude.[19] Were the function of activity appropriated by the sense drive (how, we can only imagine) a human being, Schiller claims, would "never be himself." He could never become a unity because his activity would be utterly formless. Were the function of passivity to be given to the formal drive, that man would "never be anything else,"[20] since he would not then be responsive to the particularities of sensory things. These speculations might suggest that the play drive is a fantastical creation and, consequently, that the experience it supposedly allows would be purely imaginative. Schiller, however, believes that this drive is responsible for one form of experience that is far from unfamiliar, namely, the experience of beauty. Beauty consists of both matter and form. The two fundamental drives must therefore be effective in experiences of this variety. There they work in seamless unity: matter is experienced through the form it takes, and form appears only through the material it governs. This unity is nothing less than the play drive in action.

The Play Drive and Idleness

The reconciliation of the two drives involves a new and liberating synthesis of the kinds of necessity that each imposes on us. Play, Schiller claims, "will exert upon the mind at once a moral and physical necessity [*nötigen*]; it will, therefore, since it annuls all contingency, annul all constraint [*Nötigung*] too, and set man free both physically and morally."[21] This formulation is revealing. It shows that Schiller is committed to thinking of freedom within some sense of necessity. The necessities that are reconciled look, though, to give us nothing more than a conceptual contradiction rather than a new basis for freedom. It appears that Schiller is proposing that we move from a condition in which necessity is experienced as hostile toward what we truly can be. We are not at one with current options, that is, with the shapeless promptings of the senses or the abstract discipline of formality.

But with the right kind of reconciliation, necessity can stand in harmony with "living form." What remains a difficulty, though, is why this improved condition should be marked by necessity of any kind. In annulling "all constraint" we might even suggest that human beings take on the kind of freedom that we have associated with idleness. In fact, Schiller is momentarily drawn in that direction in spite of his prudish disapproval of caprice. In the only place in the text where Schiller offers a portrait of the reality of playful behavior, he refers to the Greeks and their unsurpassable conception of harmonious life. He begins by telling us that play is "capable of bearing the whole edifice of the art of the beautiful, and of the still more difficult art of living" and describes the art of living as play thus: "Guided by the truth of that same proposition, they [the Greeks] banished from the brow of the blessed gods all the earnestness and effort which furrow the cheeks of mortals, no less than the empty pleasures which preserve the smoothness of a vacuous face; freed those ever-contented beings from the bonds inseparable from every purpose, every duty, every care, and made idleness and indifferency [*Müßiggang und die Gleichgültigkeit*] the enviable portion of divinity—merely a more human name for the freest, most sublime state of being."[22]

This passage identifies idleness and indifference to purpose as qualities of the highest form of freedom. The gods are required neither to work nor to produce. Their lives of idle play are manifestly without necessity or constraint. No identifiable norms frame their actions. Freedom from constraint or bad necessity does not appear to imply the need for a deeper, richer, or superior necessity. Schiller, though, continues: "Both the material constraint [*Zwang*] of natural laws and the spiritual constraint of moral laws were resolved in their [the Greeks'] higher concept of Necessity [*Notwendigkeit*], which embraced both worlds at once; and it was only out of the perfect union of these two necessities that for them true Freedom could proceed."[23]

This second part of the passage evidently rests on a different picture of ideal freedom. Here the necessities remain, albeit in a different form: as a speculatively stipulated higher necessity. Whatever that necessity actually means, it does not readily connect with what Schiller also attributes to the divine art of living: its idle freedom. The gods, in their "indifferency," do not care about what they are supposed to be. In this way, necessity disappears from their experience. Their behavior is without a purpose beyond itself, but it is free and, in Schiller's view, admirable. Indeed, it actually amounts to a life of "caprice" in that it is without the compulsion that comes with rational necessity. Yet it is, it seems, perfectly free. But does Schiller really want us to accept that caprice is the form of freedom—freedom from necessity—through which the highest art of living can be realized? The account of how the gods live seems to oscillate between that caprice and a supposed higher necessity that is not particularly obvious in their actions.

This tension reemerges in another form when Schiller extols the uselessness of the play state of aesthetic experience but then places that uselessness at the service of a higher necessity. He sees a resemblance between "aesthetic determinability" and "indetermination" in that "both exclude any determinate mode of existence." The absence of determinacy means, Schiller thinks, that the "aesthetic state" is commendable, as it is "completely indifferent and unfruitful as regards knowledge or character." Beauty, he continues, "accomplishes no particular purpose, neither intellectual nor moral." The sheer absence of necessity gives individuals the freedom to act in original and unconstrained directions, making of themselves what they prefer or, indeed, refraining from acting at all. In the absence of necessity we might think of the actions produced from indeterminacy as purely capricious. But Schiller then goes on to connect that indeterminacy with a kind of teleological higher necessity. The indeterminate space of freedom without necessity in fact permits the individual to "be what he ought to be."[24] Schiller may not, as Frederick Beiser claims, be "imparting any specific direction to our activity"[25] but the "ought" that comes into view, once aesthetic indeterminacy has been achieved, seems to point us in familiar directions, that is, toward another version of self-constitution.

Although what we "ought to be" is not specified in this context, the likely model for how it is to be pursued is hinted at earlier in Schiller's text. There he asserts that each of us carries within us a "pure, ideal man." It is supposedly our task to bring about a unity between all our alterations (*Abwechselungen* is the word Schiller uses) and the "unchanging unity of this ideal."[26] This unity brings together the living with the ideal. It can be established only in the context of a political entity Schiller calls the "state." He claims that the freedom that we could then enjoy would involve "wholeness of character."[27] Again, the harmony of Greek life, the reconciliation of the material and the formal is on view. Schiller does not, though, explain why wholeness—the "what he ought to be"— and the society needed to sustain it should be appealing to us.

Anthony Savile offers a supportive interpretation of Schiller's aim. Schiller's thesis, he writes, is "that men cannot rationally abjure concern for an ideal in their lives. Too often they do; but in doing so they fail of rationality." Savile believes that what Schiller is determined to establish is that it is "an a priori truth of practical reason that the Self should be formed under some concept of the good."[28] Savile here interprets the notion of "the Ideal Man" as "the good" in question. This conception of Schiller's project aligns it with the ideal of freedom as higher necessity. What this project excludes, though, according to Savile, is the choice to use one's practical reason in playful idleness: "laid back Californian spontaneity" exemplifies that abandonment.[29] If avoidance of that kind of spontaneity as the highest form of life is what Schiller intends, then we can infer that whatever action follows in this effort at self-realization will be free of caprice. Self-realization will require the serious and not evidently playful action of the complementary powers of what Schiller calls "maximum changeability and maximum extensity" together with "maximum autonomy and maximum intensity."[30]

The integration of the two basic drives means overcoming both physical and moral necessity. There is, as we have seen, something not quite compatible between this speculative systematicity and the portrait of play Schiller has presented to us. The play of the gods oscillates between idle pleasure and some immanent higher necessity that abolishes pure physical and moral necessity. That is paralleled by Schiller's account of indeterminacy, which ultimately opens us to the prospect of a teleological higher determination: rational self-realization. What is in evidence, both in the play of the gods and indeterminacy, is conceptually similar to the actions of the capricious will. And yet both moments seem to give way to a higher necessity that is in no way structurally implied in them.

What is instructive about Schiller's case is that it demonstrates the difficulty of establishing an alternative to discipline or rationalistic autonomy once we try to frame that endeavor within a theory of freedom as necessity (or some order). The latter implies an "ought." In Schiller's theory, that "ought" leads to the subordination of play to an end that lies beyond play itself. Without any sense of necessity, the notion of play becomes idleness, a notion that Schiller trades on (recall his Olympian images) without seeming to be willing to endorse its implications for the freedom and necessity relationship. In the next section, I consider Marcuse's version of the play model. He does not promote the notion of a higher necessity. Indeed, his conception of play appears to accommodate the freedom-related advantages of idleness without the hidden constraints that appear in Schiller's conception. Marcuse directly addresses the question of how work and idleness might be unified by conceiving the possibilities of work as playful idleness.

MARCUSE: WORK AS IDLENESS

In *Eros and Civilization* (1956), Marcuse enlists Schiller's notion of play to the enterprise of critical social theory. That notion, he believes, can be used to throw some light on the distorted form of everyday experience Marcuse finds in contemporary society. He maintains that our capacity for transformative and fulfilling relations with others has been replaced by purely transactional and competitive attitudes. Each party now sees in others only instrumental opportunities or threats. In this environment, the business values of the capitalist market invade all forms of social action. The routines of the worker become the habits of the private individual. Marcuse contrasts the harshness of the relentless sense of purpose that characterizes people today with the ideal form of freedom encapsulated by the notion of play. He sketches out what he thinks that notion would look like in practice. In Marcuse's work, play is not dangled before us as a tantalizing dream. He believes that a state of play is an attainable ideal for human beings. The notion of play may serve a largely critical function, in that it offers us a standpoint from which to assess current forms of experience and human relating. But Marcuse wants to convince us that that standpoint can be defended in its own terms. That is, he holds that human beings are capable—even if they are unlikely to do so—of becoming the kinds of beings who play in his sense. He employs customized versions of a variety of Freudian concepts to give substance to that capacity.

Marcuse contends that the possibility of a different kind of social relating is obscured to us by what he calls "surplus repression." Surplus repression is a species of repression that has supposedly been generated solely by "social domination." It occurs specifically in advanced capitalist societies. The main characteristics of these societies are a connection between survival and a tremendous capacity for work, the relationship between recognition and material success, and the absence of a communal sensibility. The needs of the system determine the most basic motivations of those who are socialized within it. Among the forms that surplus repression takes are, Marcuse claims, the "monogamic-patriarchal family," the "hierarchical division of labor," and "public control over the individual's private existence."[31] Freedom would become a real possibility were any one of these forms to be eliminated.

Surplus repression is to be differentiated from basic repression. Marcuse describes basic repression in Freudian sounding language as "the 'modifications' of the instincts necessary for the perpetuation of the human race in civilization."[32] These modifications bring about the reduced influence of the pleasure principle. The pleasure principle is, famously, the demand of the organism for the immediate satisfaction of desire. Just as Freud holds that adjustment of the instincts to reality entails their repression—this is

effected by the reality principle—Marcuse claims that
"surplus repression" is the effect of the "performance
principle." Under the performance principle, "society
is stratified according to the competitive economic
performances of its members."[33] Marcuse's text gives
rise to two distinct ways of understanding how this
principle relates to the reality principle. It may be understood as either the prevailing historical form of the
reality principle, or it may stand as an extra layer of
repression that, in some manner, sits above the repression of basic instincts. The repression attributable to
the performance principle, like that of the reality principle, generates neurosis. The symptom specific to surplus repression is, Marcuse writes, a "neurotic necessity" to work.[34] This necessity, we might interpolate,
has the character of a repetition compulsion: its activity is no longer consistent with its conscious objective,
that of survival.

Marcuse suggests that Schiller's conception of play
follows Kant's efforts in the *Critique of Judgment* to
find in aesthetic experience a reconciliation of freedom with nature. Kant, Marcuse notes, conceives aesthetic freedom as "lawfulness without law" and the
experience of beauty as "purposiveness without purpose." These formulations point to a variety of experience that is neither instrumental nor constrained.
Marcuse believes that such experience may also be
possible outside the aesthetic sphere. That condition
would be nothing less than what he describes as "the
free play of the released potentialities of man and nature."[35] Human beings would be free of repression,

their capacities no longer directed toward purposes that are hostile to transformative experiences. This would be, in fact, freedom from necessity. As Marcuse puts it, "Man is free only when he is free from constraint, external and internal, physical and moral—when he is controlled neither by law nor by need." A "humane civilization" of "play rather than toil" is possible only when we are freed from that neurotic necessity that compels us to perform.[36] Marcuse, as we shall see, is drawn toward images of idleness when he tries to describe experience in that civilization.

Alienated Labor

In order to understand why play is an emancipating ideal, we need to appreciate how the activity it is to supersede—work today—is perceived as a barrier to the "humane civilization" Marcuse has in mind. The problem with work is not alone that it is arduous. Rather, it is to be criticized because it is alienating. Marcuse states the basic principle as follows: "Men do not live their own lives but perform pre-established functions. While they work, they do not fulfill their own needs and faculties but work in alienation."[37] Although this statement is consistent with classical Marxist formulations, Marcuse actually departs from a key element of Marx's original version of alienated labor. For Marx, the notion of "alienated" or "estranged" labor involves the miserable experience of the production of commodities. The cause of the misery is the exclusion from that productive process of expressive-affective possibilities. Workers cannot, as we saw in chapter 2, express their distinctive personalities in the mass objects they make. Experience is diminished in that the blunted sensuousness of workers precludes the possibility of affective encounters with a complex outer world. Instead, they regard the world and its objects as standing against them as intimidating presences. The objects that result from this labor are generally distributed to distant strangers. A potentially satisfying communal purpose is absent from this form of productivity. That alienation is the source of a worker's misery is not necessarily apparent to the worker, even as the worker recognizes that the very process of labor is one in which he "does not affirm himself but denies himself." In this active self-denial, the worker, Marx says, "mortifies his body [*seine Physis abkasteit*]."[38] The discipline of the workplace makes the need for this self-denial clear to the worker. Marx, however, identifies the experience of misery as the symptom of a morbid condition: he tries to explain why work is painful. Interpretation enters the empirical world of suffering in that the true meaning of the worker's pain becomes apparent only when it is conceptualized as the effect of social arrangements.

For Marcuse, misery is not an essential attribute of alienated labor. His focus is not on the gruesome conditions of industrial production. His interest, rather, lies in that type of work that in organized societies is understood to be rewarding. Marcuse wants to interpret this apparently agreeable activity as yet another form of alienation. The focus shifts from mind-numbing, physically damaging toil and isolation to work that demands and recognizes performance. It is Marcuse's view that what our workplaces take to be effective performance will in most instances have little connection with what we could truly want for ourselves. What we actually do is to take on alien objectives as though they were our own. He writes:

> Certainly there can be "pleasure" in alienated labor too. The typist who hands in a perfect transcript, the tailor who delivers a perfectly fitting suit, the beauty-parlor attendant who fixes the perfect hairdo, the laborer who fulfills his quota—all may feel pleasure in a "job well done." However, either this pleasure is extraneous (anticipation of reward), or it is the satisfaction (itself a token of repression) of being well occupied, in the right place, of contributing one's part to the functioning of the apparatus. In either case, such pleasure has nothing to do with primary instinctual gratification.[39]

And it is because work departs from that gratification that it is, in Marcuse's view, alienated. His notion of alienated labor rests on an implicit theory of false consciousness. Among critical social theorists, this theory explains the supposed reality that individuals often construe as natural forms of social life that are both unnecessary and ultimately antagonistic to their deepest social needs. A theory that shifts the point of entry from misery to consciousness does not require itself to provide testimony from reported experience. A critical perspective built on an ideal alternative highlights deficits in the investigated phenomenon even where the phenomenon is broadly satisfying in the everyday world.

Marcuse's conception of alienated labor is designed to reach into—and critically assess—our everyday understanding of ourselves. In some of the examples we have just seen, he downplays the worth of the recognition that a worker may gain for the skillful completion of a task oriented toward another person. By many measures, including arguably Marx's, contributing to the community as a tailor or hairdresser, might be evidence of social labor, that is, of nonalienated labor. Marcuse ignores this feature of the work, though, because he seems to be committed to a notion of lower and higher pleasures. The lower version is connected with repression: it is the pleasure compatible with being a useful person within the current order of things. Higher pleasure is possible only when that order is removed. That radical state of affairs would mean the return of the "pleasure principle," the principle of gratification prior to all repression. The name Marcuse gives to pleasure in this context is "play."

Idleness and Play

Marcuse, as noted above, aligns his notion of play with the paradoxical Kantian notions of "lawfulness without law" and "purposiveness without purpose." But play is also portrayed by him as freedom from all compulsion. He writes: "The problem of work, of socially useful activity, without (repressive) sublimation can now be restated. It emerged as the problem of a change in the character of work by virtue of which the latter would be assimilated to play—the free play of human faculties. . . . Play is entirely subject to the pleasure principle. . . . 'The fundamental feature of play is, that it is gratifying in itself, without serving any other purpose than that of instinctual gratification.' "[40]

This is, implicitly, the boldest possible call for idleness. It entails complete indifference to purpose, and it makes no appeal to the notion of a self that must have integrity, moderate its desires, or find its place within a network of recognition. What is obviously puzzling about this feature of play is that it is also a model for a new concept of work. Marcuse tries to carry us toward this concept with the use of mythic figures. These figures supposedly provide evidence of human ideals that have not yet been extinguished through repression. Prometheus is given a villainous role—much as Schlegel's Julius had seen him—as he is identified as the "culture hero" of human toil.[41] In Marcuse's myth set, Prometheus is opposed by the goodly Orpheus and Narcissus, who embody human potential: ". . . [T]heirs is the image of joy and fulfillment; the voice which does not command but sings; the gesture which offers and receives; the deed which is peace and ends the labor of conquest; the liberation from time which unites man with god, man with nature." These figures, he tells us, ". . . recall the experience of a world that is not to be mastered and controlled but is to be liberated—a freedom that will release the powers of Eros now bound in the repressed and petrified forms of man and nature."[42]

To people who take their conception of normal human action from capitalist work practices, Orpheus and Narcissus are utterly bizarre. These latter live without both production and discipline. The notion of usefulness has no currency for them. Whatever form their exertions might take, it would certainly be no version of what we think of as work. Were the "life instincts" to take Orphic rather than Promethean form, Marcuse conjectures, language would become song and work would be play.[43] These words stretch the imagination. We are told that play in this sense is not, what Marcuse labels, "aestheticism," a self-indulgent break from "an otherwise repressive world."[44] What he envisages, rather, is a changed world where the norms of work and performance are nowhere to be found. It appears, in fact, that the Orphic ideal of play resonates with the life of "idleness and indifference" that Schiller attributed to the gods. Marcuse claims that play is "unproductive and useless precisely because it cancels the repressive and exploitative traits of labor and leisure; it 'just plays' with the reality."[45]

An ambivalence is evident in the claims we have just seen: work becomes play, but play is "unproductive and useless," that is, it is idleness. Marcuse sees the radically liberating implications of idleness. But he also wants to acknowledge the practical necessity of basic work. The difficulty in his position is that he attempts to accommodate both of these strands—idleness and work—within a theory of play. The strain in Marcuse's position is most evident in the various ways he struggles to explicate the place for liberated work without surrendering the notion of playful idleness. The elimination of the sphere of "surplus repression" should simultaneously eliminate work as performativity without undermining the very possibility of work. But Marcuse's Orphean ideal goes further than that: it is, as we saw, "a freedom that will release the powers of Eros now bound in the repressed and petrified forms of man and nature." This seems to say that every repressive experience that we attribute to the "reality principle" will be lifted.

Work, Play, and Idleness

How, in Marcuse's utopian future, can we meet the demand of the reality principle, that energy be diverted away from pleasure and toward practical forms of self-preservation? This might be construed as the philosophical question of whether work can be freed of the character of "necessity." In fact, Marcuse holds two main positions that are a response to this riddle: namely, minimal work and work as play.

(1) *Minimal work*. Marcuse suggests that we might actually be able to undertake minimal levels of work without compromising the libidinal transformation

he calls "play." Work will always be necessary, to a certain degree, and always essentially a violation of some kind. But once it is completed, we are left with a space for the happier business of playful idleness. As he explains, "No matter how justly and rationally the material production may be organized, it can never be a realm of freedom and gratification; but it can release time and energy for the free play of human faculties outside the realm of alienated labor."[46] In that scenario we are not quite in the Orphean world, since some continuing part of our lives must operate outside the demands of the pleasure principle. Work requires discipline, dedication to a process with which the worker is not always creatively involved. It is, as Marcuse writes elsewhere—commenting on a line from Marx's *Capital*—"the realm of necessity. The realm of necessity itself forever remains a realm of unfreedom."[47] That realm must be kept at bay: "[T]he reduction of the working day to a point where the mere quantum of labor time no longer arrests human development is the first prerequisite for freedom."[48] Marcuse then ends up reverting to the familiar question of how work and play or idleness can be balanced.

Marcuse's sensible-sounding compromise with reality is more complicated than it seems. This is because he has invested his notion of playful idleness in a quasi-Freudian psychology. He ends up with the view that human beings could plausibly live according to the pleasure principle but also have the capacity to adjust periodically to the reality principle when needs compel work. These principles, as Marcuse would have known, are hardly options to be selected as daily circumstances demand. The appearance of the reality principle, after all, dynamically alters the "self." According to Freud, "the ego is that part of the id which has been modified by the direct influence of the external world."[49] If the external world presents two realities, one of work—however minimal—and one of playful idleness, then it would appear to follow that the ego will take on a different structure in each situation. This is unlikely to be an extravagance Marcuse wants to argue for, but it looks like one to which his theory commits him.

On this point Marcuse is forced down the road of science fiction in order to escape the conflict between the reality and pleasure principles. At one stage he suggests that a solution to the conflict between work and pleasure is to take work out of the hands of human beings. Technological advances, which Marcuse tends otherwise to hold in suspicion, have brought us to the exciting possibility of "total automation."[50] Taking a lead from Marx, Marcuse imagines that machines can do what human beings will no longer be able to do, since their possible freedom from neurotic necessity would ill equip them for work.[51] As self-maintaining machines whirl away in the background, human beings would live in playful idleness. Productivity and discipline would be entirely absent from that world.

(2) *Work becomes play.* As well as trying to maintain yet harmonize separate spheres of work (in minimal

or automated form) with playful idleness Marcuse also posits the possibility of the conversion of work into play. The tension between work and freedom is in this way to be abolished. Once more the imagination is tested with this proposal. Marcuse justifies it in this context in terms again borrowed from psychoanalytic psychology: ". . . [I]f work were accompanied by a re-activation of pregenital polymorphous eroticism, it would tend to become gratifying in itself without losing its work content."[52] It looks as if, after all, that for Marcuse the complete development of human capacities is not necessarily "in irreconcilable opposition to work."[53] Eroticism entails release from the repressive influence of the reality principle but somehow without risk to self-preservation. Marcuse explains: "The altered societal conditions would therefore create an instinctual basis for the transformation of work into play. In Freud's terms, the less the efforts to obtain satisfaction are impeded and directed by the interest in domination, the more freely the libido could prop itself upon the satisfaction of the great vital needs."[54]

Here the contradictory self, acting under both pleasure and reality principles, is absent. The reconciliation, however, conceals a paradox. The "great vital needs" remain as pressing demands on our energies. Indeed, satisfying those needs is what gives the libido its direction. These demands can be met through activity that is said to be playful, but it is no longer intelligible as play in the sense of playful idleness. It now acts on specific objectives. Marcuse would later frame this possibility in nonpsychoanalytic terms. He held that technologically oriented work increasingly allowed the worker to become "supervisor, inventor and experimentor . . . subject to the free play of the mind, of imagination, the free play with the pleasurable possibilities of things and nature." The "realm of necessity"—work today—would be transformed into the "realm of freedom."[55] Play here might be analogous to game playing, in which certain objectives structure the voluntary, idiosyncratic and expressive actions of individuals. But given that Marcuse specifies that playful work can satisfy the "great vital needs," no less than the oppressive version of work, its freedom hardly meets the standard of "purposiveness without purpose." Either play takes on a purpose, in which case it is no longer play in the sense of freedom from necessity, or work becomes playful idleness, and then it is no longer work. Marcuse's theory tries to hold both of these thoughts together at once.

The complexities in Marcuse's position stem from his determination to place the notion of play at the center of a radically emancipating social theory. That notion, however, ends up bearing too much of what he envisages for a transformed society. It becomes a new concept of work, and at that point it slips from our grasp. Schiller takes a different approach to play even as he celebrates it as the essence of true humanity. Play as freedom from necessity is ultimately subordinated to a variety of different conceptions of higher necessity. In each case Schiller effectively withdraws from play the capricious quality that had seemed to recommend it.

The significance of what Schiller and Marcuse have to offer should not, though, be ignored, in spite of the marked difficulties in their handling of the idleness question. They confront the challenge that idleness is not a realistic possibility for beings like us. That leads them directly, as we have seen, to bring into doubt the value of what it is we are conventionally thought to be. If something in our present dispositions sets us against playful idleness, then we need to worry about what society has made of us. We have seen other philosophers treat our tendency to idleness as the vestige of human immaturity, evidence that the processes of gaining autonomy and achieving effective social integration are not yet complete. Schiller and Marcuse attack those very processes precisely because they are incompatible with playful idleness, which, on the contrary, notionally represents the only version of freedom that allows human beings to express themselves without deference to external or higher necessities.

CHAPTER 5

IDLENESS AS FREEDOM

There is much—as this book has tried to show—that can be disputed in the arguments of philosophers who, in various ways, put forward conceptions of life that necessarily devalue idleness. The alternatives to these conceptions, we have frequently seen, are generally painted with contempt. Efforts to escape from the various obligations we are supposed to accept means embracing childlikeness, laziness without ambition, selfishness, becoming a creature of nature, indeed a sheep. The force of these accusations comes from the connection the anti-idlers draw between their proposals and rationality. Since it is rationality that supposedly marks out human beings from the rest of nature, our self-image may be at stake when confronted with accusations of idleness in those terms. One kind of response to this is to argue that idleness is a different though perhaps more commonplace type of rationality. An argument of that sort is made by Robert Louis Stevenson. The form of idleness Stevenson has in mind

appears to be a version of the classical notion of leisure: it is opposed to business (*negotium*) because
business is the negation of productive and improving
leisure (*otium*). The claim that idleness consists "in
doing nothing" is met by him with the response that
idleness, in fact, involves "doing a great deal not recognized in the dogmatic formularies of the ruling class."
The issue, familiarly, comes down to the question of
what is to count as meaningful activity. Stevenson
wants to convince us that much that is of value is
gained outside the sphere of business. It is while playing truant on the "street"—"that mighty place of education which was the favourite school of Dickens and
of Balzac"—rather than in the formal classroom, that
the most important things can be learned. Of greater
significance to the philosophical discussion, though,
is Stevenson's suggestion that it is ceaseless diligence
that damages our capacity for experience, leaving us
with "deficient vitality." And he seems to say that the
attitude of idleness alone allows us to remain open to
experience. The idler has a "generous" spirit, is not
constrained by performance targets and set tasks, and
is not driven by the goals of the official social order.[1]

If we think of rationality as a capacity to be responsive to what is new, different, or unexpected, then
what Stevenson proposes turns out to be an original
way of defending idleness, or perhaps a rather raffish
version of leisure. His essay is not, though, about reason as such, but is a portrait of life without the limits
imposed on us by social convention. Perhaps the

greatest freedom it argues for is freedom from the
opinion of others. This release from what is expected
of us allows, what Stevenson calls, "a strong sense of
personal identity."[2] The idler feels no need to respond
to the expectations of others and consequently is not
diverted from preferred experience by hostile external
judgment. However, he perhaps goes too far in taking
possession of the prized concepts of the anti-idlers and
rewriting them in the name of idleness. Self-making of
a definite kind and rational experience are now possible with release from work, and a higher sense of self
is now achieved by a release from opinion. Indeed, in
spite of their blows at the ruling ideology of work, Stevenson's recommendations fall in with the aristocratic
notion of idleness: freedom from laboriousness and
indifference to achievement backed by an unshakable
self-belief. What this theory does not contest is the
view that there is something unacceptable about indifference to taking on an identity. It is, rather, another
way of meeting the implicitly acknowledged challenge
of self-realization.

Nevertheless Stevenson's essay offers us a useful tac-
tical way of dealing with the claims made against idleness. That tactic is to show that idleness in certain respects more successfully fulfills the very criteria of
what it means to be free than the usual moral positions that lay claim to those criteria. In what follows,
that approach will be transposed into the sphere of
philosophy in order to show that idleness can make
plausible claims as a conception of freedom (though,

as discussed at the beginning of this book, no argument that promotes idleness as a way of life will be positively developed). It is the notion of idleness as implicit resistance rather than the "vegetating" model that will be set against a number of philosophical assumptions about the proper theory of freedom.

IDLENESS AND THE
PHILOSOPHERS' FREEDOM

We have seen various philosophers maintain that idleness is a primitive or regressive form of experience. Freedom, in its sharpest contrast, is supposed to represent the self-engineered advancement of those who possess it. It is, in this way, an accomplishment rather than mere ready harmony with circumstances. This ennobling view of freedom is not, of course, shared by the idleness as boredom thesis. But that thesis does entail, in another sense, that idleness cannot either be freedom or provide the conditions for freedom. Idleness delivers us, after all, over to the supposed torment of having nothing sufficiently distracting to do. Since boredom haunts us, freedom is, if anything, for those troubled by boredom, freedom from idleness. Schopenhauer might have been pleased with the thought that human beings strive to escape from their freedom. Less grand versions of the view that boredom is a lurking danger are more likely to be satisfied with the thought that the kind of freedom we want consists in having some distracting thing of one's choosing to do.

The claim that idleness is anti-freedom does not seem, though, to be settled simply by placing it against notions of freedom that are perched on notably narrow bases. Those theories hardly overwhelm the evident appeal of idleness. For many, anticipation of idleness alone amounts to anticipation of liberation from tasks and pressures. And idleness appears to be valued because it is the actual experience of that liberation. However, as noted before, these kinds of "pathological" claims for idleness, as Kant might put it, will be received in varying ways, depending essentially on one's personal identification with work or busyness. A debate at the phenomenological level could amount to nothing more than a process of trading first-person experiences.

A more effective or at least relevant way of getting some kind of answer to the question of whether idleness can be considered as a form of freedom might be to contrast it with modern conceptions of rational self-determination. As we have seen, it is these conceptions of modern freedom that, in the name of "genuine" freedom, explicitly and programmatically denigrate the very notion of an idle person. It would therefore be significant were we to find, after the exercise of contrasts, that idleness comes closer than the classical notion of autonomy to meeting the conditions of self-direction that is a vital quality of freedom. The following contrasts will involve examining both idle freedom and a particular model of autonomy with regards to their respective capacities to accommodate a number of ideas that are uncontroversially viewed as some among the many features of freedom. (It may be that outside philosophy most of these ideas will have little credibility.) In what follows, two general issues that enhance the conceptual case for idleness will come into view. First, there is autonomy's supposed exclusive rights to certain properties of freedom. Second, is the relationship between autonomy and the quality of being at home—or fully identifying—with oneself in one's actions. Dealing with those issues will return us to some of the material that was examined in the first two chapters of this book. Here, though, that material will be presented in the form of a debate with the very notion of freedom as idleness. Before turning to the comparative work, I need to clarify briefly which idea of autonomy stands in opposition to idleness.

AUTONOMY AND EFFORT

The philosophical meaning of the word "autonomy" now ranges dramatically beyond the bounds originally intended for it. It has become, in some usages, perfectly consistent with acting irrationally, as long as the decision in a minimal legal sense belongs to the actor. That a decision is emotion-driven, mainly influenced by background conditioning, or leads to self-destruction makes it no less autonomous, according to some views. We can see that autonomy in this loosened sense should have no significant fight to pick with idleness.

With the classical version of autonomy, by contrast, idleness is pitted against a more exacting sense of freedom. That version maintains that those who are to be regarded as autonomous exercise evident conscious self-control in accordance with reasons that they themselves explicitly recognize as reasons for the self-controlling actions they undertake. Actions are identified with the "agent" under the strong criterion that they are the agent's conscious, objective, planned, and indeed self-reforming instructions to self. High levels of self-transparency, in which we know how to identify the desires we wish to control, and an attendant capacity for self-regulation appear to be required. In contrast, the experiences of idleness seem so obviously to embody meager exercises of agency. Rational self-regulation is at the basis of how we might supposedly make ourselves into creatures of outstanding worth: that is, self-legislating beings who are no longer the subjects of first or second nature. But that enterprise requires an effort that takes us away from our habitual comfort. It follows that a feature of most theories of autonomy in the exacting sense tell us, with laconic gravity, that autonomy is onerous. It is not clear that we are entitled to see ourselves as generally autonomous or autonomous in specific actions unless we have had to struggle to reach these points. In this respect autonomy has no essential relationship with happiness, though some may find some personal enjoyment in the demands it brings. And it differs from other life-affirming states of being, such as love or friendship, in which there is no pressure of disciplined self-regulation to keep ourselves to some chosen commitment.

Although struggle is a feature of a wide range of theories of autonomy, few take the same view on what the "burden" at the center of this struggle actually is. It may be, among other things, reason-governed discipline, a duty to one's potential, an obligation to reason (to getting the world right),[3] a responsibility for humanity. As we saw in chapter 1, the burdensome quality of autonomy is addressed in Kant's moral theory. He is willing to see reason exert its authority in ways that may well be disagreeable to us. And this leads—as critics as far back as Schiller have observed with horror—to a picture of human beings in which freedom necessarily involves an ongoing inner tussle. Again, this struggle could be an enduring and life-defining one, the source of constant displeasure, but nonetheless accompany action of the highest freedom. However, the worry that this model seems to involve a kind of endless oscillation between reason and desire is supposedly settled by the declaration that the self that is the self that counts is the one that identifies with reason. Hence desire loses the authority to mount a successful claim in the battle for what we really ought to want. The *auto* (self) that gives itself *nomos* (law or norms) is the *auto* for whom freedom is a question.

Few theories of autonomy explicitly endorse the reason over desire thesis in this explicit way. Nevertheless, it is a requirement of any theory influenced by Kant that we have inner resources that can be marshaled against desire.

The element of arduous demand is a continuing feature of autonomy in the exacting sense. Richard Arneson observes that "[n]ormally attainment of autonomy is an achievement, perhaps requiring heroic effort of will."[4] The language of toilsome effort is spectacularly foregrounded in Korsgaard's notion of self-constitution. The goal of all rational beings must be, she argues, to bring reason and integrity to their lives. None of these objectives are pleasing, but that does not count against them. They simply must be pursued. Korsgaard tells us that "being a person, having a personal identity, being a rational agent, is in itself a form of *work*. And the experience of *necessitation*, with its elements of effort and even of pain, is the experience of a form of *work*."[5] This forceful language, like that of Kant, is geared toward encouraging us to strengthen our "agency," our capacity to be effective with regard to the lives we make for ourselves through reflection on our beliefs and the norms around us. Those gains are what freedom consists in.

In this contention, though, one feature of freedom is emphasized over other common ones. Korsgaard, in particular, is focused on the process of liberation from what we have been up to the point of liberation. A hard-fought revolution will eventually see us overturn our tendencies to avoid what we ought to be ("a person, having a personal identity"). What is of obviously little value to this perspective is whatever comfort we enjoy through being at home with ourselves. Rather, the implementation and accomplishment of a program of self-improvement—the envisaged outcomes of which may seem far from what we currently take ourselves to be—is freedom. There is a gap between what we endorse following an exercise in objective self-reflection and the more familiar ways we figure out what we want to do, that is, by taking stock of the desires and needs we know we have. Korsgaard's position operates on the presumption that we can develop a personal identity that is rational. The identity is both unique—it is personal—and it stands behind each of our actions. It is not at the same time idiosyncratic, since it is rational and in that respect observably responsive to reasons that make sense to others who are rational. As Thomas Nagel explains, the "peculiarity" of strictly autonomous reasons "is that although they are agent-relative, they do not express the subjective autonomy of the agent at all."[6] What gives significance to idleness in this context is that it is worthwhile to those who enjoy it, in terms that refer to their own individual, subjective needs.

From the perspective of idleness, the notion of autonomy in the exacting sense involves making claims for freedom that seem to be unsettling and therefore of questionable value to freedom. Those claims ask us to depart from the familiarity we have with our own peculiar desires and motivations, that is, from our subjectivity. The advocates of muscular autonomy, for their turn, see the idleness stance as no better than an appeal to a pitiable pre-freedom where desire determines our actions. This, they believe, is nothing more than a renunciation of freedom. The difference between the two positions, at this point, involves differing temporal perspectives on what we human beings ought truly to identify with. Idle experience takes itself to be a freedom involving the whole person in present circumstances. Autonomy is a forward-looking and transformative project in which a supposed higher aspect of what we are aims to have dominion over specific decisions or perhaps our lives as a whole.

IDLENESS AND AUTONOMY

If we follow some theorists in accepting that only something like autonomy in the strict sense can provide a proper account of freedom, idleness will, as a corollary, be effectively deprived—as historically it has been—of the vocabulary that would allow it to be expressed as a form of freedom. Idleness is, after all, the inverse of everything that strenuous autonomy supposedly represents. The sharpness of the contrast, however, merely obscures some features of idleness that are perfectly compatible with acknowledged aspects of freedom.

(1) One implied contrast between idle freedom and autonomy places them respectively under the notions of negative and positive freedom. It is obvious why those burdensome versions of autonomy that require acts of self-mastery would be identified with positive freedom. Idleness, however, is misaligned with negative freedom. This is because it is not merely "freedom from" but should be understood as a positively experienced freedom from specific constraints, in particular those constraints that come from societal norms. Idleness, more accurately, is freedom in a context, a knowing indifference—and an implicit resistance—to specific recommendations about how one ought to live: the need for progress, prestige, or success through work—an integral identity, for example. And it is also the pleasure that we experience when we are free to live without those expectations. Hence, the desire for idle freedom is not a desire for a morally neutral space that can be filled as one sees fit. It is, rather, a preference for idleness itself.

In this context idleness arguably represents, in one respect, a more authentic freedom than certain theoretical versions of autonomy. Insofar as we are prepared to see the recommendations of society as painful pressures of some kind, we will interpret them as challenges to how we want to be. Autonomy, by contrast, accepts that freedom involves addressing and meeting those challenges. That was evident in the particularly stark instances of Kant's notion of usefulness and Hegel's insistence on the need for practical education as a required component of a truly free existence. There are, of course, different bases from which to react against the principle of usefulness. The values we saw associated with *Bildung*, for example, provide one notable, albeit problematic, response to the principle. The notion of idle freedom entails a life lived without effective interference in our motivations by visions of a superior version of ourselves, especially when that version is indebted to ideas of productivity and restless self-occupation. In this way, idle freedom has its content. We know in our idle freedom—where there is a conscious disregard for usefulness and its related norms—why we adopt our options, at least in the sense that we can say we are unmoved by the burdens that others are prepared to carry in the name of autonomy. We are not impressed by the belief that there is some kind of elevation in taking on those demands that autonomy might place on us. Freedom from burdens with which we do not have to identify—unless we listen to the advice of philosophers—is a standard feature of what we want an account of freedom to include. It should be stressed that the point at issue here focuses on a very specific freedom: freedom from those particular norms that are taken to gear us toward effective action in societies like ours.

(2) It is important to wrestle the notion of self-governance away from the exclusive ownership that autonomy claims over it. Like autonomy, idleness can

be conceived as a case of self-governing in the specific sense of freedom from inhibiting desire formation. According to some views of positive liberty, desire formation of that kind counts against liberty. John Christman argues that for "an individual to be self-governing it at least must be the case that she is not moved by desires and values that have been oppressively imposed on her."[7] Now what will remain openly disputable is the demarcation point between healthy socialization and oppressive socialization. Some believe that the latter involves inflicting values on individuals that contemporaneously disadvantage them relative to others in their family or social group. Healthy socialization is the more innocent business of being inevitably inculcated with the norms of the places in which we are nurtured. Diagnosis of one or the other depends on a critical perspective. And perhaps what once seemed healthy will come to look oppressive as our interpretations of things change in line with our shifting values.

But it is not actually significant from the standpoint of idleness as freedom whether there is a difference between these two forms of socialization. They both allow, after all, that we may become actors who must function in certain ways if we are to be regarded as worthy or successful, wherever that socialization takes place. Idleness as freedom might be construed as an attitude that, in the style of the Cynics, declines to be moved by those ideals that bear down on us all

within the process of social formation. And this refusal is made regardless of whether that formation has
disadvantageous or even advantageous ends to our
lives as social agents. (The classical notions of autonomy see it as offering clear benefits to us as social actors). The idler is freed from the dissatisfying need to
work for standing, to be constrained though useful.

(3) Idleness, in contrast with autonomy, seems to
have little or nothing to do with an "ethics" in even
the broadest sense. Hence, again, the inferiority of
idleness as a way of living. Now it might be thought
that this dismissive characterization is one that proponents of idleness would be pleased to accept. After
all, the lack of familiar ethical content we find in idleness gives it its distinctive look. But something may
be lost from the possibility of thinking of idleness as
freedom if this characterization is left in so bald a
form. It could mean that idleness is devoid of any
sense of a good life and as therefore some kind of in-
ertia. (Hegel's notion of the lethargic barbarian ar-
ticulates that view most vividly.) As such, idleness allegedly departs again from freedom in that it is a form
of base life that seems to involve nothing at all. It
might also suggest that idleness is a meaningless and
random course of life, as unappealing and uninterest-
ing as that which Harry Frankfurt ascribes to the
wanton. (This seems to be Korsgaard's view of those
whose preference is idleness.) In this way it would
have very little to do with freedom, since it would

involve no conscious expression of preference (not caring what one is to care about). The idler is then someone who would be indifferent to life's options. What is important here, though, is that a sense of care for what one is doing does not depend on the prior "autonomous" adoption of self-determining rules and principles. Ethics may be sufficiently understood as the process of identifying which desires we wish to act upon, though not necessarily with the constraints of thinking about their integrity-enhancing qualities nor with reference to how well our actions conform to the institutions of the world we inhabit.

Idleness cannot be defended as a form of freedom if it is no more than a life of impulse. We need not, though, reduce the options of human action to the categories of wantonness or full, rational self-determination. Between them, as it were, is the quality of what Stanley Benn, among others, identifies as "autarchy."[8] Absent from autarchy is that requirement of autonomy that we regulate our desires under principles that will both serve as rational and general rules for us and give coherence across our actions. To be autarchic, though, we will certainly see ourselves as actors, pursuing our lives as we see fit. It is perfectly possible to place idleness—and various other attitudes to life—within this tier of action. Indeed, it is not at odds with some conceptions of autonomy in the less demanding sense. Joseph Raz, for example, holds that an autonomous life is simply one that is marked by "the capacity to control and create" our own lives.[9] And in that respect, idleness does not have to be identified with wantonness. It is not a surrender to a causal story in which sensuousness and circumstances prevail. It has its own ethics in the sense of being a way of life that understands both its own needs and commitments and—in principle—that the conventional story about freedom and integration threatens those needs and commitments. The control in place does not imply a mechanism of self-denial. It is enough that we can understand what way of living matters to us. This does not secretly entail some eccentric form of strict autonomy. Its starting point is quite different from the classic model. That model portrays human freedom as a triumph in which disinclination toward reason, principles, plans of life, usefulness, and so forth are overcome. Idle freedom, by contrast, identifies with those tendencies.

The various contrasts just explored bring some conventional freedom-related concepts to the surface. We can see, perhaps, that idleness involves a sense of acting in accordance with values we take to be our own, meeting our personal understanding of what we prefer to do. It is often appreciated as freedom from pressures that seem to want to turn us into human beings of a distinctive kind, requiring us to relate to others— and indeed our own life stories—in ways that appear empty yet supposedly right. Idleness involves no inner struggle in which happiness is subordinated to some higher principle or other. The idle self is at home with itself.

It is little wonder, as noted above, that some philosophers today soften the burdens of autonomy, eliminating its emphasis on the preeminence of objective reason and the systematic integrity of our selves in the conduct of our lives and our self-understanding. In this new context, perhaps, no denigration of idleness need even be implicit. The case for idleness is a different matter. It will depend on whether questions of freedom can be asked without framing the answers within notions of the type of people required by modern societies. The implications of such a shift are not insignificant. They point to the implausible-sounding scenario in which the phenomena of usefulness, competitive social identities, or long-term discipline no longer form the outlines of our experience. A reappraisal of idleness is, in this respect, also criticism of those notions of freedom that work in favor of life determined in those ways.

NOTES

INTRODUCTION

1. I am sympathetic to a rejection of the idea that criticism must be constructive for the additional reason set out by Geuss, namely, that it burdens the critic into silence. See Raymond Geuss, *A World without Why* (Princeton, NJ: Princeton University Press, 2014), chap. 4.

2. William Morris, "Signs of Change," in *The Collected Works of William Morris*, ed. Mary Morris (Cambridge: Cambridge University Press, 1915), 23:20.

3. As Hume put it in the advertisement for the volume in which this essay appears, *Essays, Moral and Political* (1741).

4. David Hume, "The Epicurean," in *The Philosophical Works of David Hume* (Edinburgh: Adam Black and William Tait, 1826), 3:157–59.

5. Hume, "The Epicurean," 3:160–61. Hume nevertheless winks at an intimate sensuousness through the figure of Caelia.

6. Hume famously claims that "there is a great uniformity among the actions of men, in all nations and ages, and that human nature remains still the same, in its principles and operations" (David Hume, *Enquiries concerning Human Understanding and concerning the Principles of Morals*, ed. L. A. Selby-Bigge and P. H. Nidditch [Oxford: Clarendon Press, 1975], 83).

7. Friedrich Schlegel, *Lucinde, and the Fragments*, trans. Peter Firchow (Minneapolis: University of Minnesota Press, 1971), 63, 65, 66, 65, 68 (emphasis added), 65.

8. Jean-Jacques Rousseau, *The Confessions*, in *The Collected Writings of Rousseau*, ed. Christopher Kelly, Roger D. Masters, and Peter G. Stillman; trans. Christopher Kelly (Hanover, NH: University Press of New England, 1995), 5:537.

9. David James, *Rousseau and German Idealism: Freedom,*

Dependence and Necessity (Cambridge: Cambridge University Press, 2013), 204.

10. Jean-Jacques Rousseau, *Emile, or on Education*, in *The Collected Writings of Rousseau*, trans. and ed. Christopher Kelly and Allan Bloom (Hanover, NH: University Press of New England, 1995), 13:187.

11. Pentti Ikonen and Eero Rechardt, *Thanatos, Shame and Other Essays* (London: Karnac, 2010), 28.

12. Sigmund Freud, "The Economic Problem of Masochism," in *The Standard Edition of the Complete Psychological Works of Sigmund Freud*, ed. James Strachey, Anna Freud, Alix Strachey, and Alan Tyson (London: Vintage, 2001), 19:160.

13. Martha Nussbaum, *The Fragility of Goodness: Luck and Ethics in Greek Tragedy and Philosophy*, 2nd. ed. (Cambridge: Cambridge University Press, 2001), 449.

CHAPTER 1. OUR WORTHINESS FOR FREEDOM

1. Jean-Paul Sartre, *Existentialism and Humanism*, trans. Philip Mairet (London: Methuen, 1948), 29, 30.

2. Christine M. Korsgaard, *Self-Constitution, Agency, Identity, and Integrity* (Oxford: Oxford University Press, 2009), 69.

3. Robert Burton, *The Anatomy of Melancholy*, ed. Thomas C. Faulkner, Nicolas K. Kiessling, and Rhonda L. Blair (Oxford: Oxford University Press, 1994), 3:445.

4. Burton, *The Anatomy of Melancholy*, ed. Thomas C. Faulkner, Nicolas K. Kiessling, and Rhonda L. Blair (Oxford: Oxford University Press, 1989), 1:6.

5. Burton, *Anatomy of Melancholy*, 1:238.

6. A useful survey of the perceived consequences of idleness among moralists in the century prior to Burton can be found in Ann Wagner, "Idleness and the Ideal of the Gentlemen," *History of Education Quarterly* 25, nos. 1/2 (1985): 41–55.

7. Burton, *Anatomy of Melancholy*, 1:240.

8. Robert Burton, *The Anatomy of Melancholy*, ed. Nicolas K. Kiessling, Thomas C. Faulkner, and Rhonda L. Blair (Oxford: Oxford University Press, 1990), 2:68.

9. Burton, *Anatomy of Melancholy*, 1:240.

10. Burton, *Anatomy of Melancholy*, 2:68.

11. Burton, *Anatomy of Melancholy*, 2:84, 90.

12. Seneca, "De otio," in *Moral Essays*, trans. John W. Basore, Loeb Classical Library (Cambridge, MA: Harvard University Press, 1932), 2:189, 195.

13. Burton, *Anatomy of Melancholy*, 1:302 and passim, 2:95, 1:241. Burton, we can see from his text, recommends the study of the great writers and the important sciences. That material is absorbing and distracting. It appears, though, that the possibility of a more just society must not be drawn from that study, a conclusion quite in contrast to Seneca's.

14. Burton, *Anatomy of Melancholy*, 1:122.

15. Jean Calvin, *Institutes of the Christian Religion*, trans. Henry Beveridge (Peabody, MA: Hendrickson, 2008), bk. 3, chap. 8, sec. 5, p. 460.

16. This is outlined in some detail in Richard Adelman, *Idleness, Contemplation and the Aesthetic, 1750–1830* (Cambridge: Cambridge University Press, 2011), chap. 1.

17. Adam Ferguson, *Principles of Moral and Political Science*, quoted in Adelman, *Idleness*, 21.

18. Immanuel Kant, "An Answer to the Question: 'What Is Enlightenment?,'" in Kant, *Political Writings*, ed. Hans Reiss (Cambridge: Cambridge University Press, 1991), 58, 54, 58.

19. Immanuel Kant, "Idea for a Universal History with a Cosmopolitan Purpose," in Kant, *Political Writings*, p. 43.

20. Kant, "Idea for a Universal History," 43.

21. Kant, "Idea for a Universal History," 44.

22. Kant, "Idea for a Universal History," 45.

23. Josef Pieper also notes Kant's insistence on effort as the means of achieving truth (Pieper, *Leisure: The Basis of Culture*, trans. Alexander Dru [London: Collins Fontana, 1965], 26–27). Kant makes that claim in his critique of enthusiastic philosophy, a philosophy that believes truth can be immediately gained through feeling. Pieper opposes Kantian work with leisure, but by leisure he ultimately means contemplation and prayerfulness. In some respects his notion of leisure corresponds with the notion of idleness pursued in this study, even though Pieper wishes to expose

idleness as an inferior form of experience (cf. 42–43), but ultimately his notion is subordinate to a purpose rooted in categories of metaphysical transcendence.

24. Kant, "Idea for a Universal History," 44.

25. Kant, "Idea for a Universal History," 45.

26. Kant, "Idea for a Universal History," 46. Though a further metaphor seems to doubt this straightness of line: "Nothing straight can be constructed from such warped wood as that which man is made of" (ibid., 46).

27. Immanuel Kant, *Groundwork of the Metaphysics of Morals*, trans. Mary Gregor (Cambridge: Cambridge University Press, 1997), 31.

28. Kant, *Groundwork*, 32.

29. Immanuel Kant, *Critique of Practical Reason*, trans. Mary Gregor (Cambridge: Cambridge University Press, 1997), 69, 71.

30. Kant, *Groundwork*, 59.

31. Kant, *Groundwork*, 32–33.

32. Kant, *Groundwork*, 33.

33. Kant, *Groundwork*, 33.

34. Reinhart Koselleck, *The Practice of Conceptual History: Timing History, Spacing Concepts*, trans. Todd Samuel Presner et al. (Stanford, CA: Stanford University Press, 2002), 176.

35. Wilhelm von Humboldt, *The Limits of State Action*, trans. J. W. Burrow (Cambridge: Cambridge University Press, 1969), 17.

36. Frederick C. Beiser, *The Romantic Imperative: The Concept of Early German Romanticism* (Cambridge, MA: Harvard University Press, 2003), 92.

37. Humboldt, *Limits of State Action*, 80.

38. Rudolf Vierhaus, "Bildung," in *Geschichtliche Grundbegriffe*, ed. Otto Brunner, Werner Conze, and Reinhart Koselleck (Stuttgart: Klett-Cotta, 1972), 1:519.

39. Quoted in W. H. Bruford, *The German Tradition of Self-Cultivation: "Bildung" from Humboldt to Thomas Mann* (Cambridge: Cambridge University Press, 1975), vii.

40. E. Lichtenstein, "Bildung," in *Historisches Wörterbuch der Philosophie*, ed. Joachim Ritter (Basel: Schwabe, 1971), 1:925.

41. Hans Weil, *Die Entstehung des deutschen Bildungsprinzips* (Bonn: H. Bouvier und Co. Verlag: 1967), 266.

42. Johann Wolfgang von Goethe, *Wilhelm Meister's Apprenticeship and Travels*, trans. Thomas Carlyle, 3 vols. (London: Chapman and Hall, 1874), 1:195, 196.

43. Goethe, *Wilhelm Meister's Apprenticeship and Travels*, 1:209.

CHAPTER 2. WORK, IDLENESS, AND RESPECT

1. Thorstein Veblen, *The Theory of the Leisure Class: An Economic Study of Institutions* (London: George Allen and Unwin, 1925), 43.

2. Bertrand Russell, *In Praise of Idleness and Other Essays* (Abingdon: Routledge, 2004), 8.

3. Leo Tolstoy, *War and Peace*, trans. Amy Mandelker (Oxford: Oxford University Press, 2010), 522.

4. G.W.F. Hegel, *Phenomenology*, trans. A. V. Miller (Oxford: Oxford University Press, 1977), 80.

5. Hegel, *Phenomenology*, 116.

6. Hegel, *Phenomenology*, 116.

7. Hegel, *Phenomenology*, 117, 118, 119.

8. Hegel, *Phenomenology*, 118–19.

9. Alexandre Kojève, *Introduction to the Reading of Hegel: Lectures on the Phenomenology of Spirit*, ed. Raymond Queneau and Allan D. Bloom; trans. H. J. Nichols (Ithaca, NY: Cornell University Press, 1980), 20.

10. G.W.F. Hegel, *Philosophy of Right*, ed. Allen W. Wood; trans. H. B. Nisbet (Cambridge: Cambridge University Press, 1991), § 188, p. 226.

11. Hegel, *Philosophy of Right*, § 189, p. 227.

12. Hegel, *Philosophy of Right*, § 192, p. 229.

13. Hegel, *Philosophy of Right*, § 190A, p. 229.

14. Hegel, *Philosophy of Right*, § 192A, p. 230.

15. Hegel, *Philosophy of Right*, § 190, p. 228.

16. Hegel, *Philosophy of Right*, § 194, p. 230.

17. Hegel, *Philosophy of Right*, § 194, p. 231.

18. Hegel, *Philosophy of Right*, § 195A, p. 231.

19. Hegel, *Philosophy of Right*, § 195A, p. 231.

20. Hegel, *Philosophy of Right*, § 197, p. 232.

21. In lectures that preceded the publication of the *Philosophy of Right*, Hegel notes, "The poor man feels as if he were related to an arbitrary will, to human contingency, and in the last analysis what makes him indignant is that he is put into this state of division through an arbitrary will. Self-consciousness appears driven to the point where it no longer has any rights, where freedom has no existence" (quoted in the editorial notes to Hegel, *Philosophy of Right*, 453).

22. Indeed, back in the *Phenomenology*, Hegel speaks about usefulness in less approving terms. When considering the disruptive effects on "faith" produced by the Enlightenment, he worries that we have reduced ourselves merely to utility. We try to make all aspects of the world useful to us, and this includes making ourselves useful. He says, with some concern, that in these times it is the "vocation" of each person "to make himself a member of the group, of use for the common good and serviceable to all. The extent to which he looks after his own interests must also be matched by the extent to which he serves others, and so far as he serves others, so far is he taking care of himself: one hand washes the other. But wherever he finds himself, there he is in his right place; he makes use of others and is himself made use of" (Hegel, *Phenomenology*, 342–43).

23. Sarah Jordan, *The Anxieties of Idleness: Idleness in Eighteenth-Century British Literature and Culture* (Lewisburg, PA: Bucknell University Press, 2003), 138. Jordan argues that where industry became a supreme virtue, it was thought not to be a wrong to compel the idle to work, up to and including slavery. Hegel certainly does not entertain exploitation, even though his views of the non-industrious people of the exotic world are consonant with the conventional wisdom of his times.

24. Hegel, *Philosophy of Right*, § 197, p. 232.

25. Hegel writes, "Poverty in itself does not reduce people to a rabble; a rabble is created only by the disposition associated with poverty, by inward rebellion against the rich, against society, the government, etc. It also follows that those who are dependent on contingency become frivolous and lazy [*arbeitsscheu*], like the *laz-*

zaroni of Naples, for example" (*Philosophy of Right*, § 244A, p. 266).

26. Rousseau, curiously, went even further. The right kind of practical education will ensure that we will never idle, even when we are utterly free—as Rousseau's Emile is supposed to be—from the need for social recognition. The right habituation to manual labor, Rousseau notes, "counterbalances . . . the idleness which would result from his indifference to men's judgments and from the calm of his passions . . . (Jean-Jacques Rousseau, *Emile, or on Education*, in *The Collected Writings of Rousseau*, trans. and ed. Christopher Kelly and Allan Bloom [Hanover, NH: University of New England Press, 1995], 13:353).

27. Roland Paulsen, *Empty Labor: Idleness and Workplace Resistance* (Cambridge: Cambridge University Press, 2014), 175.

28. What Marx has to say about idleness in the later *Capital* is more straightforward and does not need to be critically examined within the framework of this study. In that text he repeatedly brings to our attention the self-evident unacceptability of a system that leaves one class with the freedom to idle while another must labor under the most abysmal circumstances. In this context, idleness has a direct connection with exploitation, a connection that an assortment of capitalist propagandists cited by Marx, attempt to justify.

29. Karl Marx, "Comments on James Mill, *Elémens d'économie politique*," in Karl Marx and Friedrich Engels, *Collected Works* (London: Lawrence and Wishart, 1975), 3:224.

30. Marx, "Comments on James Mill," 3:227.

31. Marx, "Comments on James Mill," 3:227–28.

32. Karl Marx and Friedrich Engels, *The German Ideology*, in Marx and Engels, *Collected Works*, 5:217.

33. Marx and Engels, *German Ideology*, 5:218.

34. Marx and Engels, *German Ideology*, 5:218.

35. John Dewey, *Democracy and Education*, in *The Middle Works of John Dewey 1899–1924*, ed. Jo Ann Boydston (Carbondale, IL: Southern Illinois University Press, 2008), 9:265.

36. Marx and Engels, *German Ideology*, 5:218.

37. Marx and Engels, *German Ideology*, 5:218.

38. Karl Marx, *The Poverty of Philosophy: Answer to the Philosophy of Poverty by M. Proudhon*, in Marx and Engels, *Collected Works* (London: Lawrence and Wishart, 1976), 6:142.

39. Marx, *Poverty of Philosophy*, 6:142.

40. Marx, *Poverty of Philosophy*, 6:142.

41. Marx, *Poverty of Philosophy*, 6:142.

42. Marx, *Poverty of Philosophy*, 6:142.

43. Karl Marx, *Outlines of the Critique of Political Economy*, in Marx and Engels, *Collected Works* (London: Lawrence and Wishart, 1986), 28:529–30.

44. Karl Marx, *Economic and Philosophic Manuscripts of 1844*, in Marx and Engels, *Collected Works* (London: Lawrence and Wishart, 1975), 3:274.

45. Marx, *Outlines of the Critique of Political Economy*, 28:532.

CHAPTER 3. THE CHALLENGES OF BOREDOM

1. Immanuel Kant, *Anthropology from a Pragmatic Point of View*, trans. Robert B. Louden (Cambridge: Cambridge University Press, 2006), 43.

2. Patricia Meyer Spacks, *Boredom: The Literary History of a State of Mind* (Chicago: University of Chicago Press, 1995), 9.

3. Thomas Goetz et al., "Types of Boredom: An Experience Sampling Approach," *Motivation and Emotion* 38 (2014): 403–4.

4. Lars Svendsen, *A Philosophy of Boredom*, trans. John Irons (London: Reaktion Books, 2005), 41–42. Svendsen draws, in this instance, on the work of Martin Doehlemann.

5. Peter Toohey, *Boredom: A Lively History* (New Haven, CT: Yale University Press, 2001), 4.

6. P. James Geiwitz, "Structure of Boredom," *Journal of Personality and Social Psychology* 3, no. 5 (1966): 593. Geiwitz is reporting the view of J. E. Barmack.

7. Reinhard Kuhn, *The Demon of Noontide: Ennui in Western Literature* (Princeton, NJ: Princeton University Press, 1976), 12. One of Maria Edgeworth's narrators asks, "Among the higher classes, whether in the wealthy or the fashionable world, who is unacquainted with *ennui*?" (Edgeworth, *The Novels and Selected*

Works of Maria Edgeworth, ed. Jane Desmarais, Tim McLoughlin, and Marilyn Butler [London: Pickering and Chatto, 1999], 1:162).

8. As one study puts it, "Rather than fighting boredom we would do well to pause and learn from the experience. From the psychodynamic perspective, the experience of boredom is important because it provides an opportunity to discover the possibility and content of one's desire" (J. D. Eastwood et al., "A Desire for Desires: Boredom and Its Relation to Alexithymia," *Personality and Individual Differences* 42 [2007]: 1043).

9. Toohey, *Boredom*, 174.

10. Arthur Schopenhauer, *The World as Will and Representation*, trans. E.F.J. Payne (New York: Dover Publications, 1969), 1:364, 164, 322.

11. Schopenhauer, *World as Will and Representation*, 1:260.

12. Schopenhauer, *World as Will and Representation*, 1:375. Similarly, when willing and desire seem to be synonyms, "[t]he basis of all willing, however, is need, lack, and hence pain" (ibid., 1:312).

13. Schopenhauer, *World as Will and Representation*, 1:315.

14. Schopenhauer, *World as Will and Representation*, 1:313.

15. Arthur Schopenhauer, *The World as Will and Representation*, trans. E.F.J. Payne (New York: Dover Publications, 1966), 2:492.

16. Schopenhauer, *World as Will and Representation*, 1:318.

17. Schopenhauer, *World as Will and Representation*, 1:313–14.

18. Bernard Reginster, "Schopenhauer, Nietzsche, Wagner," in *A Companion to Schopenhauer*, ed. Bart Vandenabeele (Malden, MA: Wiley Blackwell, 2012), 352.

19. Schopenhauer, *World as Will and Representation*, 1:260. And: "For desire and satisfaction to follow each other at not too short and not too long intervals, reduces the suffering occasioned by both to the smallest amount, and constitutes the happiest life" (ibid., 314).

20. Schopenhauer, *World as Will and Representation*, 1:313.

21. Arthur Schopenhauer, *Parerga and Paralipomena*, trans. E.F.J. Payne (Oxford: Oxford University Press, 1974), 1:331, 332.

22. Schopenhauer, *Parerga and Paralipomena*, 1:331, 332.

23. Ivan Soll, "Schopenhauer on the Inevitability of Unhappiness," in Vandenabeele, *A Companion to Schopenhauer*, 307. We might note that the confusion is not due to the similarity of the words, since in German they are *Befriedigung* and *Sättigung*.

24. Schopenhauer, *World as Will and Representation*, 1:313.

25. Schopenhauer, *World as Will and Representation*, 1:325.

26. Schopenhauer, *World as Will and Representation*, 2:444.

27. Schopenhauer, *World as Will and Representation*, 2:152.

28. Schopenhauer, *World as Will and Representation*, 2:154.

29. Schopenhauer, *World as Will and Representation*, 2:154.

30. Friedrich Nietzsche, *Human, All Too Human*, trans. R. J. Hollingdale (Cambridge: Cambridge University Press, 1996), § 611.

31. Nietzsche, *Human, All Too Human*, § 283.

32. Nietzsche, *Human, All Too Human*, § 291.

33. Søren Kierkegaard, *Either/Or*, trans. David F. Swenson and Lillian Marvin Swenson (Princeton, NJ: Princeton University Press, 1959), 1:285.

34. Kierkegaard, *Either/Or*, 1:285.

35. Simone de Beauvoir, *The Second Sex*, trans. H. M. Parshley (London: Jonathan Cape, 1953), 157.

36. Beauvoir, *Second Sex*, 157.

37. Beauvoir, *Second Sex*, 268n.

38. Beauvoir, *Second Sex*, 562.

39. Beauvoir, *Second Sex*, 663.

40. Beauvoir, *Second Sex*, 562.

CHAPTER 4. PLAY AS IDLENESS

1. Bertrand Russell, *In Praise of Idleness and Other Essays* (Abingdon: Routledge, 2004), 11.

2. Friedrich Schiller, *On the Aesthetic Education of Man in a Series of Letters*, trans. Elizabeth M. Wilkinson and L. A. Willoughby (Oxford: Clarendon Press, 1967), letter 6, p. 35.

3. Schiller, *Aesthetic Education*, letter 4, p. 21.

4. For an account of Schiller's worries, throughout his philo-

sophical writings, about the "despotic" nature of moral law, see R. D. Miller, *Schiller and the Ideal of Freedom: A Study of Schiller's Philosophical Works with Chapters on Kant* (Oxford: Clarendon Press, 1970), 51–54.

5. Schiller, *Aesthetic Education*, letter 4, p. 21.

6. Beiser neatly expresses this difference: "*Kant subordinates humanity to morality whereas Schiller subordinates morality to humanity*" (Frederick C. Beiser, *Schiller as Philosopher: A Re-examination* [Oxford: Clarendon Press, 2006], 186).

7. Schiller, *Aesthetic Education*, letter 3, p. 11.

8. Schiller, *Aesthetic Education*, letter 15, p. 107.

9. Schiller actually holds two views of where play stands in relation to higher necessity. Higher necessity is directly manifest in actual aesthetic/play experience (play is fulfilled freedom), but it also has a teleological status in that it is a necessity that becomes evident to those human beings who have learned how to play in Schiller's sense (play alerts us to moral freedom). Eva Schaper sees this ambivalence in the very idea of aesthetic education itself: "[I]t is not altogether clear when Schiller speaks of 'aesthetic education' whether it is education *to* the aesthetic, understood as the ideal state for man to attain, or *through* which ordinary living can be enhanced" (Schaper, "Towards the Aesthetic: A Journey with Friedrich Schiller," *British Journal of Aesthetics* 25 [1985]: 156).

10. Schiller, *Aesthetic Education*, letter 11, p. 77.

11. Schiller, *Aesthetic Education*, letter 15, p. 101.

12. Schiller, *Aesthetic Education*, letter 3, p. 165.

13. Schiller, *Aesthetic Education*, letter 12, p. 79n (translation changed).

14. Schiller, *Aesthetic Education*, letter 13, p. 85.

15. Schiller, *Aesthetic Education*, letter 7, p. 46.

16. Schiller, *Aesthetic Education*, letter 4, p. 17.

17. Schiller, *Aesthetic Education*, letter 3, p. 13.

18. Schaper, "Towards the Aesthetic," 164.

19. Schiller, *Aesthetic Education*, letter 13, p. 89.

20. Schiller, *Aesthetic Education*, letter 13, p. 89.

21. Schiller, *Aesthetic Education*, letter 14, p. 97.

22. Schiller, *Aesthetic Education*, letter 15, p. 109.

23. Schiller, *Aesthetic Education*, letter 15, p. 109.

24. Schiller, *Aesthetic Education*, letter 21, pp. 145–47.

25. Beiser, *Schiller as Philosopher*, 155.

26. Schiller, *Aesthetic Education*, letter 4, p. 17.

27. Schiller, *Aesthetic Education*, letter 4, p. 23.

28. Anthony Savile, *Aesthetic Reconstructions: The Seminal Writings of Lessing, Kant and Schiller*, Aristotelian Society Series 8 (Oxford: Basil Blackwell, 1987), 205. Savile acknowledges (on 208n) that this account of Schiller may seem to be "fanciful" but corroborates it with reference to claims found elsewhere in Schiller's writings.

29. Savile, *Aesthetic Reconstructions*, 205.

30. Schiller, *Aesthetic Education*, letter 13, p. 87.

31. Herbert Marcuse, *Eros and Civilization: A Philosophical Inquiry into Freud* (London: Routledge and Kegan Paul, 1956), 37–38.

32. Marcuse, *Eros and Civilization*, 36. Freud famously writes, "Under the influence of the ego's instincts of self-preservation, the pleasure principle is replaced by the reality principle" (Sigmund Freud, *Beyond the Pleasure Principle*, in *The Standard Edition of the Complete Psychological Works of Sigmund Freud*, ed. James Strachey, Anna Freud, Alix Strachey, and Alan Tyson [London: Vintage, 2001], 18:10).

33. Marcuse, *Eros and Civilization*, 44.

34. Marcuse, *Eros and Civilization*, 211. The phrase "neurotic necessity" is quoted by Marcuse from C. B. Chisholm's *The Psychiatry of Enduring Peace and Social Progress*.

35. Marcuse, *Eros and Civilization*, 177. On this point Marcuse diverges from Schaper's tenable claim that anyone "who looks for a deliberate continuation of the thought of the *Critique of Judgment* [in Schiller's text] . . . looks in vain" (Schaper, "Towards the Aesthetic," 157). Schaper seems to be on safer ground by heeding Schiller's own statement on the absence of any systematic connection between his theory and Kant's.

36. Marcuse, *Eros and Civilization*, 187, 188.

37. Marcuse, *Eros and Civilization*, 45.

38. Karl Marx, *Economic and Philosophic Manuscripts of 1844*, in Karl Marx and Friedrich Engels, *Collected Works* (London: Lawrence and Wishart, 1975), 3:274.

39. Marcuse, *Eros and Civilization*, 220–21.

40. Marcuse, *Eros and Civilization*, 214. The last sentence is a quote from Barbara Lantos.

41. Marcuse, *Eros and Civilization*, 161.

42. Marcuse, *Eros and Civilization*, 162, 164.

43. Marcuse, *Eros and Civilization*, 171.

44. Marcuse, *Eros and Civilization*, 188.

45. Marcuse, *Eros and Civilization*, 195.

46. Marcuse, *Eros and Civilization*, 156.

47. Herbert Marcuse, "The Realm of Freedom and the Realm of Necessity: A Reconsideration," *Praxis: A Philosophical Journal* 5 (1969): 22.

48. Marcuse, *Eros and Civilization*, 152.

49. Sigmund Freud, "The Ego and the Id," in *Standard Edition*, 19:25.

50. Marcuse, *Eros and Civilization*, 156.

51. Marcuse notes both his debt to Marx and the fact that Marx did not adhere to this speculative solution (Marcuse, "Realm of Freedom and the Realm of Necessity," 22).

52. Marcuse, *Eros and Civilization*, 215.

53. Morton Schoolman, "Further Reflections on Work, Alienation, and Freedom in Marcuse and Marx," *Canadian Journal of Political Science / Revue canadienne de science politique* 6, no. 2 (1973): 302.

54. Marcuse, *Eros and Civilization*, 215.

55. Marcuse, "Realm of Freedom and the Realm of Necessity," 23–24.

CHAPTER 5. IDLENESS AS FREEDOM

1. Robert Louis Stevenson, *An Apology for Idlers* (1877; London: Penguin, 2009), 1, 4, 7, 8.

2. Stevenson, *Apology for Idlers*, 7.

3. John McDowell, "Autonomy and Its Burdens," *Harvard Review of Philosophy* 17 (2010).

4. Richard J. Arneson, "Freedom and Desire," *Canadian Journal of Philosophy* 15 (1985): 434.

5. Christine M. Korsgaard, *Self-Constitution, Agency, Identity, and Integrity* (Oxford: Oxford University Press, 2009), 26.

6. Thomas Nagel, *The View from Nowhere* (Oxford: Oxford University Press, 1986), 181.

7. John Christman, "Liberalism and Individual Positive Freedom," *Ethics* 101, no. 2 (1991): 345.

8. Stanley Benn, *A Theory of Freedom* (Cambridge: Cambridge University Press, 1988), 152 ff.

9. Joseph Raz, *The Morality of Freedom* (Oxford: Oxford University Press, 1986), 408.

INDEX